WARTIME SHIPYARD

A Study in Social Disunity

KATHERINE ARCHIBALD

With a new introduction by
**ERIC ARNESEN AND
ALEX LICHTENSTEIN**

University of Illinois Press
Urbana and Chicago

Library of Congress
Cataloging-in-Publication Data
Archibald, Katherine, 1916–
Wartime shipyard : a study in social disunity /
Katherine Archibald ; with a new introduction
by Eric Arnesen and Alex Lichtenstein.
p.   cm.
Originally published:
Berkeley : University of California Press, 1947.
Includes bibliographical references and index.
ISBN-13: 978-0-252-07386-1 (pbk. : alk. paper)
ISBN-10: 0-252-07386-x (pbk. : alk. paper)
1. Shipbuilding workers—United States.
2. Shipyards—United States. I. Title.
HD8039.S52U52   2006
331.7'62383097309044—dc22   2006006959

WARTIME SHIPYARD

CONTENTS

ACKNOWLEDGMENTS

❧ WE WOULD LIKE *to acknowledge the following institutions and individuals for their assistance.*

Florida International University for a research travel grant; University of Illinois at Chicago for research and travel support; Rice University and University of Illinois at Chicago for financial support for photo reproduction and indexing; Bill McMorris at the Oakland Museum of California for help identifying Dorothea Lange's photographs; the San Francisco Public Library for sending us a copy of an interview done with Ray Thompson; the Bancroft Library at the University of California, Berkeley; the Labor and Archival Research Collection at San Francisco State University; Robert Cherny; Brian Kelly, Daniel Letwin, Ruth Milkman, Monica McCormick, and the anonymous readers who vetted our proposal and introduction for the Press; Archie Green for a stimulating and impromptu oral history occasioned by a chance encounter in the archives; and Joan Catapano at the University of Illinois Press. Special thanks to Lara Kriegel and Katrin Schultheiss for all their support.

For all our children: Hannah, Rachel, Sam and Will, and Max, in descending order of birth.

INTRODUCTION

"All Kinds of People"
ERIC ARNESEN AND ALEX LICHTENSTEIN

A Liberal Intellectual
Amongst the Working Class

"The white folks had sure brought their white to work with them that morning." So mused Bob Jones, the African American protagonist of Chester Himes's 1945 novel of West Coast wartime shipyard labor, *If He Hollers Let Him Go.*[1] Himes's fictional account of the ever-present racial tension in the shipyards of San Pedro, California, told in the voice of a black worker, resonates with Katherine Archibald's dismayed observation that the typical white shipyard worker she encountered at Oakland's Moore Dry Dock shipyard bore a racial hatred that represented "an indispensable constituent of his sense of well-being." Himes's novel explored the dramatic encounter of a racially divided working class thrown together in a great mass production industry stimulated by World War II from the perspective of an embittered African American. By contrast, *Wartime Shipyard*, Archibald's contemporaneous ethnographic depiction of the same phenomenon, appeared in the form of an "objective" piece of social science designed to explore what she called, in language far less pungent than Himes, the "problem of social disunity."[2]

Disunity indeed was a problem of great concern to social scientists in the 1930s and 1940s, one made all the more pressing by economic depression, the rise of fascism in Europe, and, after Pearl Harbor, the exigencies of wartime sacrifice and cooperation on the home front. Katherine Archibald, and many young intellectuals like her, greeted this world with a mixture of fear and hope that informed both their study of social problems and their faith in solutions to the manifest ills of their time. If Archibald's generation confronted economic crisis and racial conflict at home and fascism and world war abroad, the tools to defeat these evils also seemed at hand: an activist liberal state, a revivified trade union movement, an ethic of pluralism and diversity, and the American ideals of equality and democracy, for which fascism would be no match (or so they hoped).

Wartime mobilization tested these ideals. Successful prosecution of the war required a virtually unprecedented national effort, involving every sector of American society. The production of military equipment—ships included—involved a large and heterogeneous collection of people assembled together into a cohesive force. The question of home front unity attracted considerable attention from the military and civilian government officials, industrialists, and trade union leaders, who all aggressively promoted wartime patriotism and encouraged unanimity of purpose on the part of the nation's diverse civilian population. "We are all kinds of people," declared the company magazine for the enormous Kaiser shipyards in Richmond, California in 1944. "We are of every color—black and white, yellow and red—and of every faith—Catholic and Protestant, Jewish and Mohammedan. Some of us are young, some old, and some of us are hale and hearty, some crippled and handicapped. . . . But whatever we are or were, we get along fine, working side by side. Americans all, we know it takes all kinds of people to build ships. . . . Shoulder to shoulder, we'll come through together."[3]

Katherine Archibald did not doubt that the war effort required unity; she further believed that in the peace that was to follow, the very "future of man depends on the emergence and maintenance of inclusive social unities."[4] Archibald's book, first published in 1947 by the University of California Press, reflected both her training as a sociologist and the liberal ethos of its day. Born in Seattle in 1916, she had gone to high school in Hollywood and attended the local University of California, Los Angeles. Then, between 1938 and 1942, she studied in the Bay Area at the University of California, Berkeley's Department of Social Institutions, where she received her Ph.D. A precursor to Berkeley's distinguished sociology department, social institutions provided a multidisciplinary and liberal education that immersed Archibald in the study of history, social theory, psychology, and economics. Her three principal advisors at Berkeley included Margaret Trabue Hodgen, a sociologist and economist who wrote about (among other things) women in industry and trade unions, and who had published an educational pamphlet for the YWCA entitled *Factory Work for Girls* (1920); Robert H. Lowie, a cultural anthropologist who had studied with Franz Boas, who no doubt introduced Archibald to the ethnographic method she would put to good use as a "proficient eavesdropper" in the shipyard; and Leo Rogin, a Marxist economist. Thus, when she arrived at Moore Dry Dock after four years of graduate study, in June 1942, Archibald likely brought with her an interest in women and work, a grasp of radical economic theory, and training in anthropological fieldwork and relativist (and thus antiracist) cultural anthropology. Together, these tools of analysis allowed her to develop a point of view remarkably prefigurative of the intellectual preoccupations of social historians half a century later. *Wartime Shipyard* offers an unusual window into what today would be called the dynamics of class, race, gender, and ethnicity.

In the absence of more than a few scraps of Archibald's personal papers or reminiscences, however, it remains unclear why she decided to work in the shipyard. Certainly she did not intend to conduct fieldwork for her dissertation on "The Literature of African Voyage and Exploration," which she completed in June 1944.[5] But her assiduous note taking suggests she regarded her shipyard sojourn as a form of social research not incompatible with her academic training. Nevertheless, Archibald's subsequent career appears only tangentially related to the research she conducted during the war. After teaching as an instructor in Stanford University's history department between 1945 and 1950, she moved on to Pomona College in southern California where her husband Charles H. George was also a professor. Now known as Katherine George, she remarked with some irony that "Our patriarchal customs can make for a fair amount of confusion where the professionally minded female is concerned."[6]

In the following years she taught at the University of Rochester and the University of Pittsburgh, before finally settling with her husband in Winnipeg, Canada, where she taught the sociology of religion at the University of Manitoba. Indeed, her academic work focused on the question of social hierarchy in religious thought, and she eventually co-authored a number of works on the history of religion with her husband.[7] In fact, this work may not have been as far afield from her wartime concerns as it appears at first glance. In her 1950 article on social hierarchy in the thought of St. Thomas Aquinas, Archibald concluded that in his thirteenth-century world view, "society is essentially a hierarchy" with a "leisured elite ruling over a dull-witted and sodden-souled mass of manual workers . . . because the mass is presumably incapable of managing itself." One wonders how far this Thomist vision really departed from Archibald's own observations during her time at Moore Dry Dock. In a subsequent letter to another scholar, she described *Wartime Shipyard* as "an analysis of the hierarchical structure of a society of shipyard workers."[8]

Perhaps this life-long intellectual focus on the dynamics of hierarchy and social dominance came from the eye-opening experience of working in the shipyard. As Archibald admitted, prior to her arrival at Moore Dry Dock she was a rather typical liberal academic of the time: theoretically sympathetic to the working class while almost entirely unaccustomed to mingling with members of that class. Her scholarly training and her liberal political sympathies led her to believe that workers' common interests and common status would lead to "some sense of unity" and that the "common people" would bear responsibility for advancing society toward a "equalitarian and universalistic goal." Such notions reflected not only the regnant ideas at Berkeley in the 1930s and 1940s, but also a popular faith in the "common people" that animated social activists, government planners, artists, writers and intellectuals in the New Deal Era.[9] Her two-year stint as a worker-observer at Moore Dry Dock, however, proved many of her preconceptions false, revealing a world that completely belied the Kaiser company's claim of "Americans all." What Archibald found were "social abysses so deep that the possibility of spanning them never occurred, apparently, to right-minded people . . . I found intolerance of slight linguistic and cultural differences so great that the ghosts of feudal snobbery seemed to have come alive."[10]

Mobilizing for War

Few moments in American history did more to open up and reveal those "social abysses" beneath a surface unity than did life on the home front during World War II. Yes, Americans left behind the Great Depression with a newfound unity of purpose—to defeat the Axis powers. And wartime mobilization and production in the "arsenal of democracy" put an end to the unemployment that had bedeviled the American economy for over a decade. At the same time, however, Americans experienced what historian David Kennedy calls the "great wartime demographic reshuffling," as millions—indeed, one-fifth of the entire population—left the familiarity of home to enter military service or migrate to a defense job during the forty-four months the nation was at war. Eight million people headed for the Pacific coast.[11] "By 1943," historian of California Kevin Starr writes, "the United States was at war with itself as well as with the Axis powers. The mobilization of American society for war was bringing into close contact disparate groups of Americans who feared, distrusted, even hated each other. No where was this more true than in California."[12] Men and women drawn from isolated rural and farm communities suddenly found themselves living in congested urban areas, punching a clock, and working in enormous industrial plants with tens of thousands of other workers drawn from all over the country. Southern whites and southern blacks, long habituated to a rigidly defined set of customary behaviors dictated by white supremacy, encountered one another in entirely new workplaces and social settings, riding integrated streetcars to work, for example. Men and women brought up to believe inflexibly in their respective roles as breadwinner and homemaker had to reorient themselves to sharing the industrial workplace as co-equals, a difficult adjustment for both sexes. And small suburban communities like Richmond, California (population twenty-three thousand) transformed into industrial cities with one hundred thousand people virtually overnight when a war plant was set down in their midst.[13]

Richmond, ten miles north of Oakland's Moore Dry Dock yards on the shore of the East Bay, was home to the Kaiser shipyards, which employed upwards of ninety thousand workers at the peak of wartime production. In fact, the Kaiser yards and the urban community they engendered, rather than nearby Moore Dry Dock, were the subjects of the Dorothea Lange photographs Archibald chose to illustrate her book. As Lange recognized, the defense industry's transformation of Richmond was emblematic of the profound impact the expansion of the wartime shipbuilding industry had on California in general and the San Francisco Bay area in particular.[14] Between 1940 and 1946 California's labor force increased by 40 percent, swelled by an influx of 1.6 million workers into the state to work in defense-related industries. Like hundreds of thousands of other men and women in wartime California, if for different reasons, Archibald gravitated to the burgeoning shipyards of the state's coastal industrial entrepôts. As she remarked, "ships had to be built." The lucrative "cost-plus" defense contracts that undergirded the construction of ships were part of the $35 billion spent by the Federal government in the state between 1940 and 1946.[15] The hunger for labor at the area's shipyards seemed insatiable, drawing not only women and African Americans but also high school students, the elderly, and the handicapped. As one Kaiser manager put it, employers looked "under the railway bridges and into the jails for workers."[16] The six thousand shipyard workers in the Bay Area in 1939 swelled to two hundred and forty thousand at the peak of wartime employment, as shipbuilding employed nearly eighty percent of those engaged in heavy industry in the area. Half of these new shipyard workers could be found at Kaiser Shipyards and Moore Dry Dock, which itself grew from employing six hundred to well over thirty thousand workers.[17]

Despite Archibald's claim that the wartime shipyard in which she worked was "representative of them all," in some ways, Moore Dry Dock was atypical.[18] Unlike the Kaiser and Marinship "instant shipyards" up the bay in Richmond and Sausalito, constructed expressly for wartime production, Moore's had been building ships since before World War I. Founded in 1905 by Joseph A. Moore, his son Robert S. Moore, and John Scott as the Moore & Scott Iron Works, this family-based firm secured war contracts in the First World War and built thirty ships for the government under the name Moore Shipbuilding Company.[19] Unlike many shipyards, Moore's remained competitive after World War I, especially in the growing market for oil tankers, and even diversified by entering the fabrication of structural steel. Ship production halted during the Depression, but government contracts for steel bridgework remained.[20]

In abandoning the construction of "dry cargo" ships, Moore Dry Dock was not alone; only two were built in the United States between 1922 and 1937. In 1936, only ten shipyards in the entire country had the capacity to build 400–foot plus vessels. But government action resuscitated American shipbuilding in the closing years of the Great Depression. In an effort to modernize the country's merchant marine fleet, Congress passed the Merchant Marine Act of 1936. The Act created the U.S. Maritime Commission (USMC), a government agency tasked with providing subsidies to American shipyards to help make them competitive with European shipbuilders. Under Vice Admiral Emory Scott Land, the USMC would take a proactive role during the war and become central to the wartime procurement of cargo ships that could transport materiel to the European and Pacific theaters.[21]

Moore Dry Dock secured its first USMC contract even before the war began, in December 1938. Three years later, with wartime demand for ships booming, the company expanded its facilities to include more "building slips, a steel fabricating shop, machine shop, pipe shop, mold loft, shop cranes and cranes to serve the building slips, machine tools, plate fabricating equipment, and an office building." At the time, in 1941, only four thousand people worked at Moore Dry Dock; by 1943, that number had grown to thirty-seven thousand. According to the company history written half a century later, "no shipyard in the country was saddled with a more difficult or complicated workload than Moore Dry Dock Company." Second only to the enormous Kaiser yards, where upwards of ninety thousand workers built over seven hundred ships, Moore Dry Dock produced one hundred vessels during the war.[22]

Thus the wartime shipyard Katherine Archibald entered in the summer of 1942 "as an academician and a liberal," but posing as a worker, had some particular features. It was an "old-line" yard, which meant that a small core of experienced workers would have to accommodate themselves to the influx of vast numbers of newcomers. The established skilled workers at Moore would also have to adjust to the increased specialization, heightened division of labor, and deskilling that came with a sudden increase in production and manpower. Unlike the Kaiser yards in Richmond, around which an entirely new urban community grew virtually overnight, Moore Dry Dock sat in an already established urban area, the city of Oakland. Finally, Moore's was not a large, corporate contractor which, like Kaiser or Bechtel (the owner of Marinship), took up shipbuilding because it was a profitable form of wartime production. Instead, the company was a family firm with a "hands-on management style" that had always built ships, and expanded to meet wartime demand.[23]

A World of Caste and Class

Her book's title notwithstanding, Archibald's perceptive ethnographic eye focused less on a wartime shipyard as a physical site for the organization of production than on "the people who during a war worked in a shipyard, and the attitudes they cherished." What she saw surprised and depressed her. At the heart of the worldview of the white male majority she found a "vision of society as hierarchically constituted"; in this world of "class and caste," various groups were arranged in order of their superiority to inferiority. Male shipyard workers might maintain a "formality and politeness" toward their female coworkers, but "a half-concealed resentment still persisted" against them as "rivals of men in a man's world." Toward the "Okies," those white migrants from Oklahoma, Texas, Missouri, and Arkansas, white shipyard workers, male and female, erected "barriers of distrust and discrimination" and expressed ridicule at their dialect, ostensibly flamboyant dress and manner, and alleged stupidity. Whites expressed contempt for the Portuguese and hatred toward the Japanese who had been interned in military camps. Deeply anti-Semitic, white shipyard workers disdained the small number of Jews working in the shipyard, characterizing them as loan sharks, shysters, union-breakers, capitalists, the "grinders of

the faces of the poor," grafting politicians, and embezzlers. Occupying the bottom of the white shipyard
worker's "order of races," African Americans found
themselves despised by most whites (including the
"Okies"), who attributed to them a predatory sexuality (imperiling white women), an inherent biological and moral inferiority, incompetence in their craft,
disease, and a fervent desire to displace whites from
their higher economic positions and to achieve social
equality. "Thus even the most ignorant white shipyard
worker whose post was at the bottom of a thousand
higher steps," Archibald concluded, "might by virtue
of racial heritage alone look arrogantly down upon his
black-skinned companions in toil."[24]

The gulf between Archibald's understandings of
race, aided no doubt by her work at Berkeley with
anthropologist Robert Lowie, and the conceptions
held by those in her study was extremely wide. In the
two decades before World War II, anthropologists,
biologists, psychologists, and sociologists radically
revised their thinking on race, rejecting earlier scientific endorsements of hierarchies of multiple races
and notions of innate racial inferiority. This "scientific repudiation of racism," in Elazar Barkan's words,
involved not merely the decline in the respectability
of "racial-biological perspectives" but their replace-
ment by an emphasis on the impact of environment
and culture on group behavior. As a liberal student
of anthropology in the early 1940s, Archibald would
have taken this "repudiation of racism" for granted.[25]

But popular racial thinking lagged behind the latest paradigmatic shifts in scientific and social scientific scholarship. Clinging to interpretive frameworks that prevailed since the late nineteenth century, Moore Dry Dock's white workers ranked different groups—the "Teutonic, Scandinavian, or Anglo-Saxon stock," Okies, the Portuguese, Jews, and African Americans—in a descending "order of races" (or "hierarchy of scorn") and ascribed to them stereotyped characteristics that proved remarkably impervious to "logic or fact." In insisting upon the biological and cultural inferiority of African Americans, white shipyard workers undoubtedly shared with the vast majority of white Americans deeply held prejudices that liberal academics and left-wing activists had done little to eliminate. It was Archibald's liberal thinking on race, not her subjects', that was held by a distinct minority, even by the 1940s.[26]

Archibald's academic preconceptions of shipyard workers' views clashed with reality in two additional areas. The first was "class consciousness," of which she found little. Expecting to find both the "factual unity of labor's interest" and labor's awareness of that unity, she instead encountered particularistic resentments and a profound fatalism. Workers were aware of class distinctions, of course, and resented the possessors of excessive wealth (particular Jews), but they accepted "hierarchical society as natural, eternal, and inevitable." "There was always a boss," they believed, and it was workers' fate to follow the boss's orders.

Acceptance of hierarchy did not mean an acceptance of an individual worker's place within it. Many a male worker hoped that somehow, fate (though not hard work, thrift or investment, the pursuit of education, or even ability) might catapult them to wealth. Shipyard workers' resentment of their bosses and the rich, however, never evolved "into resentment against a distinct class of exploiters or expropriators and against the hierarchical system which sustained them"; they advanced "no vision of an equalitarian society" and translated none of their grievances into "an integrated policy of rebellion."[27]

Nor did shipyard workers appear swept up in any wave of wartime patriotism or nationalism. Although many purchased war bonds and expressed hatred of the Japanese enemy (they were less hostile toward the Germans), Moore Dry Dock workers expressed little interest in the war's purpose, revealing a skepticism that the function of official ideologies of wars were to obscure "a naked selfishness and lust for power" by those waging them. Few if any men volunteered to enlist in the military and many expressed antagonism toward Great Britain and the Soviet Union, both wartime allies of the United States. Archibald identified as the "substance of shipyard patriotism" a "simple pride in the nation's vigor, certainty of its victory, and a rousing hatred of its enemies." Shipyard workers' cynicism toward wartime ideology and government officials extended even to the realm of electoral politics, toward which many demonstrated a widespread

indifference on the grounds that politicians were corrupt and that politics had little effect on their personal affairs. The well-studied working-class support
for President Franklin D. Roosevelt and his New Deal
was in little evidence at Moore Dry Dock.[28]

Yet Archibald was not dispirited by everything she
encountered during her tenure as a shipyard worker. Among Moore's white male workforce, especially
those with skills, she never met a man who was "essentially servile or broken in spirit," for their "pride
in themselves and their capacities was strong." Archibald was impressed with an "atmosphere of comradeship and intimacy" she encountered as a white
woman, and she was favorably impressed with her
immediate work group's generous spirit of mutual
aid, manifested in their collection of funds for those
injured, whose wives were ill, and the like. Face-to-
face relations were largely friendly, extending even
to some women and "Okies." While "shipyard generosity never crossed the barrier between black and
white," blacks and whites "cooperated in countless
tasks, white shoulders straining beside black." And
of the many prejudices Archibald encountered on the
job, she admitted that they were "for the most part
merely verbal in their substance," rarely translating
into physical attacks against ostracized groups. If
such prejudices were "far from shallow, temporary, or
purposeless," she believed that under other circumstances "they might have been weakened and diverted
as utterly to have lost their force for evil."[29] Her regret

was that the potential for social unity remained unrealized in the postwar era.

For all of its ethnographic interest in shipyard workers and their worldviews, *Wartime Shipyard* is remarkably silent about the world outside of the shipyard gates. Archibald apparently restricted her search for class consciousness and social unity to her hours on the job. Little in her study reflects on her subjects' homes or the communities they inhabited, their commutes to and from work, their religious beliefs and practices, their encounters with mass culture, or their daily struggles to make lives for themselves and their families before and after their work shifts. Had she looked outward to Oakland and the larger East Bay to observe closely the fabric of life in the "boomtowns" around her, she might have uncovered further empirical evidence to explain the very social disunity that her academic and political perceptions had ill prepared her to find.

Katherine Archibald's Oakland—and indeed, the entire San Francisco Bay area—experienced radical changes during World War II. "The sweeping war production program has affected virtually every segment" of the region's economy as early as 1942, the year Archibald joined the Moore Dry Dock labor force, one contemporary study revealed; the following year, Oakland city manager Charles R. Schwanenbert concluded that the "impact of war activity in Oakland has revolutionized the economy of the entire east bay area." These observers were hardly exaggerating.

In the space of a few short years, the region became *the* premier shipbuilding center in the entire United States, drawing between four and five billion dollars in contracts from the U.S. Maritime Commission and the U.S. Navy. Accompanying the dramatic growth of shipyards was a concomitant and voracious appetite for labor. Shipyards were "ravenous for men," Archibald observed, and they "absorbed them all." But they quickly discovered that the Bay Area could hardly supply the vast numbers their machinery of production required. Shipyard companies engaged in aggressive recruitment drives, luring newcomers with promises of steady work at good wages. Their efforts were made easier by the arrival of a much larger number of voluntary migrants to the Bay Area, men and women who came on their own, leaving their homes in the South or Southwest in search of a better life, better opportunities, or simply a better job.[30]

In the absence of coordinated federal or state planning and investment, the arrival of so many newcomers to the Bay Area placed a severe strain on local resources and generated social tensions. Local officials were simply unprepared for the scale of the inmigration and financially unable to meet the growing cost of services. Housing represented the most severe problem, with the local housing market incapable of absorbing so many people and too little federally constructed housing to make a substantive difference. Some workers secured housing in company-constructed barracks; others lived considerable distances from their workplaces, commuting up to two hours in each direction each day; still others doubled up with friends, relatives, or strangers in a single apartment or were forced to live in trailers or tent camps; many were actually homeless, sleeping in public parks or their cars. Whatever the specifics of their situation, most shipyard workers lived in "shipyard ghettos," geographically separated from older residents of Oakland or other Bay Area communities, who looked down upon the newcomers as lazy, socially inferior, and the source of social problems. What was true of shipyard workers as a group was even more true of African American shipyard workers, who were largely excluded from white neighborhoods of older residents and new arrivals alike by vigilant anti-black property owners' associations, restrictive covenants, strictly observed social practices, and, in the case of company housing or federal housing projects, were segregated from whites by official rules. "The great majority of Negroes concentrated in West Oakland, North Oakland, and West Berkeley," concluded one 1943 study, "live under slum conditions . . . adjacent to manufacturing and the docks. Houses are old and run-down. Vice and crime are prevalent."[31]

The wartime housing crisis was only the most immediate and visible of the problems confronting the Bay Area. Only with considerable difficulty did primary and secondary schools imperfectly absorb the growing number of out-of-state children of shipyard workers. Local officials complained that the huge

numbers of military and worker migrants generated
"police, health, and sanitation problems beyond the
ability" of municipalities to solve. Rising crime and
delinquency rates plagued communities; "wholesome"
recreation facilities proved scarce; and inadequate
transportation systems not only added excessive travel
times to work but also contributed to low morale, high
labor turnover, and inefficiency in production. While
the East Bay experienced no major bloody race riots
on the order of the Detroit riot or racially motivated
hate strikes as drastic as the Alabama Dry Dock strike
in Mobile, both occurring in 1943, racial conflict between blacks and whites sometimes assumed the form
of physical clashes, both in the yards and in the larger
communities. By 1943, historian Gerald Nash has concluded, "utter chaos prevailed in the cities of the Bay
Area and threatened a very real breakdown of war
production."[32]

A vast influx of newcomers from across the country,
high rates of labor and residential turnover, a severe
housing crisis, residential segregation by class and
race, inadequate municipal resources, and sharp competition for goods and services—these were hardly
auspicious circumstances for achieving social unity or
cohesiveness of any kind. Even had shipyard workers' common experiences promoted a workplace class
consciousness as Archibald's academic theories had
predicted, that unity would have been undercut by
shipyard workers' varied expectations, backgrounds,
and cultures, on the one hand, and the harsh mate-

rial conditions and structural constraints they encountered, on the other. "In the war boomtowns—in
contrast to many permanent working-class communities," historian Marilynn S. Johnson has argued in her
study of the wartime East Bay, "the familial quality
of defense worker households did not translate into
a wider communal ethos." The growth of a strong
community ethos or common culture was hindered
by "long hours, staggered shifts, high turnover, and
a general sense of temporariness and anonymity." As
one Richmond shipyard worker recalled, "Everybody
was coming and going at different times. I was never
around enough to really know any neighbors." The
absence of much intergroup cooperation, however,
did not mean individual migrant groups experienced
only anomie or lacked any sense of internal cohesion.
Throughout the East Bay, various groups of migrants
created their own subcultures and community institutions—churches, bars, stores, community centers,
and theaters. But the ethnic and racial fragmentation
that Archibald observed inside the shipyard was rep-
licated outside of it as well. As in the shipyard, there
were no social forces or institutions able or willing
to unite the heterogeneous populations of East Bay
communities.[33]

"Ships for Victory" on the Assembly Line

If there was a potential countervailing force to the
rampant disunity Archibald observed all around her,
she sought it first in the shipyard trade unions. The

plural form is used because myriad American Federation of Labor (AFL) craft organizations dominated many organized West Coast shipyards. As Archibald recognized, locals of the Steamfitters (to which she belonged), the Pipefitters, and the International Brotherhood of Boilermakers, Iron Shipbuilders and Helpers (the Boilermakers), to name but three, followed AFL tradition and chose to protect the narrow interests of a self-defined elite of skilled workers—traditionally white and male—rather than seek a broader basis of solidarity. As Archibald suggests, the shipyard craft unions affiliated with the AFL proved ill equipped to engage in political education of the swelling ranks of their membership during the war. And, in fact, most established AFL members had no desire to incorporate the newcomers into their organization in any meaningful way, other than as dues payers. The failure to do so represented an important missed opportunity to build and sustain the legitimacy of trade unionism in the aftermath of the Great Depression and the war.

In many wartime shipyards elsewhere in the country, AFL unions met a formidable challenge from the recently formed "industrial" shipbuilders' union affiliated with the Congress of Industrial Organizations (CIO), the Industrial Union of Marine and Shipbuilding Workers of America (IUMSWA). Unlike their craft union rivals, IUMSWA organizers welcomed the masses of unskilled and uninitiated workers with open arms into a single, unified organization without craft divisions. By 1944 IUMSWA had built an impressive and diverse organization of 218,100 workers, with especially strong concentrations in the Atlantic Coast yards.[34] But the industrial union failed to make inroads in the Bay Area, leaving the field to AFL unions like the Boilermakers, which proved much less receptive to the masses of new workers pouring into the shipyards.

The massive influx of labor went hand in hand with another threat to the position of the skilled trades: the reorganization of production, most dramatically in "overnight" shipyards like Kaiser, but at Moore Dry Dock as well. The wartime necessity to build merchant and transport ships faster than enemy submarines could sink them put a premium on efficiency, part standardization, and speed in shipyard construction. "Urgency encouraged innovation, and new techniques of . . . assembly-line production were developed to turn out ships in record time. Only a nation fully mobilized for war could have successfully mounted a heroic effort of this sort," notes maritime historian Arthur Donovan.[35] Just as Henry Ford had done for the mass production of the automobile a generation before, at the behest of the Maritime Commission Henry Kaiser now applied the technique of assembly line and the minute division of tasks to the building of ships. "We are not only building ships," the Chairman of the USMC told Congress, "we are assembling ships. We are more nearly approximating the automobile industry than anything else." In fact, the head of production at the Kaiser shipyards, Clay

Bedford, visited one of Ford's factories and came away with the determination to implement a similar division of specialized labor in the shipyard then springing to life in a corner of the East Bay.[36]

The central manufacturing advances to this end in wartime shipyards were *prefabrication* and *pre-assembly*. In the past, an entire ship might be built from the ground up as a single unit after the keel had been laid on the shipyard way. During the wartime emergency, however, the widespread use of ship parts fabricated elsewhere meant that "work traditionally done on the ways was now performed outside the yard so that all that remained to be done was to put the parts together." In order to avoid parts bottlenecks, the largest shipbuilding yards, like Kaiser, turned to the technique of preassembly. This innovative form of integrated shipyard production allowed the various components of a ship, from steel hull plates to bulkheads to deck housing, to be fabricated and assembled separately in the shipyard itself and then lifted by cranes to the way for final construction. "The wartime demand for ships created a new unprecedented style in shipbuilding because it was an unprecedented demand," wrote Frederic Lane, the historian commissioned by the Maritime Commission to prepare its history after the war.[37]

This reorganization of production, which went unremarked by Archibald, had some important implications for the fractious social relations she observed in the shipyard. Most significantly, the expansion of pre-

fabrication broke down many of the skills shipbuilding craftsmen had traditionally guarded jealously, so
that job classifications became simpler and far more
numerous. This, of course, permitted workers who
had never been in a shipyard before to acquire rapidly the technical expertise to do a particular assembly task—welding, for example, a less skilled task that
came to supplant riveting, and in which many women
were employed.[38] Skilled tasks that had once required
years of apprenticeship now could be learned in a
matter of weeks. Frederic Lane noted that fifty percent of the workers in prewar ship construction "were
skilled workers in the sense that they had served an
apprenticeship of four years" and learned a craft that
required mastery of between forty and seventy skilled
operations. Now, in yards organized to build ships
with prefabricated and preassembled components,
many workers could start work as soon as they had
mastered one task. "The new methods of construction
made it possible to draw on all parts of the nation's
manpower, and womanpower, to carry on one of the
most difficult of industries," Lane concluded in his
Ships for Victory. As a result, "actual construction of
the world's largest merchant marine was the handiwork of farmers, shopkeepers, housewives, and workers recruited from every walk of life."[39]

Because of the absolute necessity of converting almost overnight to wartime mass production of ships,
these innovations could be said to have helped win the
war. They made it possible to train and incorporate

huge numbers of unskilled migrant workers—including blacks and women, long denied access to shipyard production jobs—in a short time. But for the shipyard trade unions of the AFL, the Boilermakers in particular, this represented a profound challenge to their control over work assignments, labor training, job classification, and the production process itself. At the same time, "closed shop" agreements approved and protected by the government assured the union loads of new members, a prospect embraced only reluctantly by the established membership. By 1943 the Richmond Boilermakers' Local 513 alone had swelled to 36,511 members—more than the entire *national* membership of the Boilermakers' Union only five years before![40]

Structurally, much of the internal tension around shipyard labor can be attributed to this Faustian bargain struck by the shipyard craft unions. At the close of the war, Local 513 published *Richmond: Arsenal of Democracy*, a history of the union's wartime experience that suggested the degree of ambivalence established West Coast shipyard craft unions had about their astounding wartime expansion. On the one hand, the union bemoaned the fact that the newcomers "knew little or nothing about unions or union procedure, and unfortunately didn't want to learn." At the same time, embracing the language of wartime unity, *Arsenal of Democracy* boasted of its membership that "each and every one [is] an American, organized in as perfect a union shop as has yet been devised, working and sweating to preserve our way of life and the rights of the oppressed peoples of the world." Finally, explaining their resistance to allowing the neophyte shipyard workers much of a voice in the union's affairs, the Boilermakers pointed out that their "membership was as diversified in background, knowledge of trade unionism, and opinion, as the kernels of corn in the average cornfield. Nothing but internal strife would have prevailed had this great mass of new members, uninitiated in the trade unionism movement, exercised control."[41]

Prefabrication and preassembly, then, are key factors in understanding the dynamics of rapid shipyard expansion, the incorporation of masses of newcomers inexperienced in industrial work, and the consequent hostility of the established shipyard craftsmen to their arrival. But just who were the new workers greeted by their fellows with such an unwelcome reception? In Archibald's account they fall largely into three categories, which we will consider in turn: women, Okies, and African Americans.

"Wendy the Welder"

When the United States entered the war in late 1941, a quarter of the nation's women already worked for wages outside their own homes (although the figure for black women was far higher—thirty-eight percent—than for white). But only 15.5 percent of married women did so.[42] The number of women employed expanded from twelve million in 1940 to nineteen million by 1945, peaking at a labor force participation figure of thirty-six percent. This was not simply a market response to the huge labor demand stimulated by wartime output and labor shortage. Federal governmental agencies did much to encourage female labor force participation, from recruitment and training (the War Manpower Commission), to propaganda (the Office of War Information), and even, in a few rare instances, the provision of child care for female defense workers with young children (Federal Works Agency).[43]

Despite the ubiquitous image of "Rosie the Riveter,"[44] the attractive, can-do woman manufacturing worker who appeared in wartime propaganda, the seven thousand women who worked with Archibald at Moore Dry Dock represented but a small percentage of the overall number of women who poured into the wartime labor force. At the peak of female employment, two million women worked in defense plants, but this never represented more than ten percent of all women workers at the time. Shipyard employment was indeed one of the largest categories of female industrial employment during the war (second only to aviation), but the total in this industry never exceeded two hundred and twenty-five thousand. And only a small number of women broke into the skilled trades in any industry; less than five percent of war jobs classified by the government as skilled went to women, and even fewer to African American women, who were only hired into these positions late in the war, if at all.[45]

The new role for women as industrial workers was simultaneously embraced and denied, understood as an act of patriotic duty and yet accommodated to the feminine ideals to which most of the society, including women themselves, continued to adhere. A promotional booklet published by Marinship emphasized the personal sacrifice women made for their men when they entered the shipyard. "Forsaking homes, professional careers and easy peacetime jobs to tackle the rugged life of a shipbuilder," it intoned, "many of these women have a double stake in helping to win the war quickly, for they have husbands, fathers, sons or sweethearts overseas with the fighting forces."[46] An article in the *Woman's Home Companion* could report with pride that "American women are learning how to put planes and tanks together, how to read blueprints, how to weld and rivet and make the great machinery of war production hum under skillful hands and eyes," yet insist at the same time that "they're also learning how to look smart in overalls and how to be glamorous after work. They are learning to fulfill both the useful and the beautiful ideal."[47] When not adhering to the "beautiful ideal," women workers were portrayed as continuing what we might call the "domestic ideal." One wartime newsreel, entitled "Glamour Girls of 1943," reassured those who doubted women's capacity for skilled manufacturing work with these words: "Instead of cutting the lines of a dress, this woman cuts the pattern of aircraft parts. They are taking to welding as if the rod were a needle and the metal a length of cloth to be sewn. After a short apprenticeship, this woman can operate a drill press just as easily as a juice extractor in her own kitchen."[48]

Archibald's description of women shipyard workers reflected her own experience with the hostility of her male co-workers. By the summer of 1943, a year after she arrived, twenty percent of the thirty-five thousand workers at Moore Dry Dock were women. (Women were well represented at the Kaiser yards as well, where by 1944 they constituted nearly a quarter of all production workers, and seventy percent of all laborers, the least skilled classification in the yard. Though less able to secure positions in the skilled trades because of opposition from the unions, they also made up forty-one percent of all welders, and thirty-three percent of all burners at Kaiser.)[49] Archibald's ambivalent portrait of the woman shipyard worker can be supplemented by the stories that appeared in the shipyard newsletters that appeared in the Bay Area. Produced by management, publications like Kaiser's *Fore 'n Aft* and Marinship's *The Marin-er* and *The Stinger* trumpeted the skill, dedication, and diversity of their work forces (unfortunately, no comparable publication for Moore's seems to be available). They often highlighted the contributions of women workers with a mixture of praise and condescension. *The Stinger* ran a special column by Marinship's "Women's Counsellor" (not an uncommon official hired by shipyards during the war, including Moore's) explaining why "Gals Take Time

Off." Sick children, lack of child care, and difficulty shopping—all of which remained working women's domestic duties, despite their long hours—were held to blame, not the women themselves. "Richmond Shipyards have established a corps of specialists to help smooth the transition of the housewife, the office worker, the traditional career woman into the ship-building technician in a strange new world of unaccustomed grime, noise, and machinery," reported *Fore 'n Aft*, even while the company's "Women's Coordinator" assured "Women are not competing for men's jobs—they are patriotically taking the places of men called into the armed forces."[50]

Issues like workplace safety took on new meanings when women entered the shipyards. One number of *The Marin-er* opened its pages to a "debate" about "who are the safer workers." Mary McNulty, a trainee, insisted "men are bad housekeepers. They let everything accumulate in a mess until there is an accident," while "women are used to looking after the safety of the whole family." Not so, countered Marvin Geister, a Marinship control engineer. "Most women may learn how to use a tool," he admitted, "but they never completely understand it. They are not mechanically inclined—and the accident figures give the proof. . . . They are mighty ornamental, but they just aren't built for safety" he proclaimed. The shipyard's superintendent of safety played the referee; not surprisingly, he concluded evenly "if you will wear proper safety clothing for your job, if you will observe the reasonable safety rules—there is no reason why a man or a woman need ever have a serious accident."[51]

Though never addressed directly in such company newsletters, in Archibald's account the greatest fear among men in the yards was of female sexuality. Archibald argued persuasively that the sexual rumors and innuendos that held sway in the shipyard functioned to express a more general displeasure with female encroachment into a previously all-male work environment. Rumors aside, however, Archibald claimed that many of the shipyard women in fact did see the yard as a highly sexualized space; but here Archibald had little sympathy for the freedom this may have granted many women. The conditions of wartime boomtowns, with large transient populations of in-migrants and servicemen, and an increasing number of unattached (even if only for the duration) young people of both sexes, opened up the possibility of sexual freedom for many women, single and married, for the first time. Evidence uncovered by Marilynn Johnson in her research on wartime Oakland suggests that many young women took advantage of this situation and sought casual sexual encounters. No doubt the shipyards, like the aircraft plants of southern California workplaces now shared by men and women, were not immune to the changing sexual mores of wartime, as Archibald admitted.[52] The eroticization of wartime social space proved especially explosive when mixed with the dry tinder of racial tensions.

Surprise surprise

Like many of her contemporaries Archibald saw
little progress in breaking down long-standing gender barriers and attitudes, which seemed impervious
to the upheavals of the war. "The unprecedented relationships between men and women which wartime
work entailed . . . were to be in large part reabsorbed
into the dominant pattern of tradition," she remarked
with evident disappointment.[53] In the closing years of
the war, the Women's Bureau of the U.S. Department
of Labor conducted a survey of thirteen thousand
women workers in ten of the nation's largest "war
production areas," including the Bay Area, in order to
determine their postwar employment plans. The subsequent report noted that "an unprecedented increase
occurred during the war in the number of women employed," having more than doubled between 1940 and
1945 in eight of the ten areas studied. In the San Francisco area, for example, 137,000 women had joined the
labor force, swelling their numbers to 275,000, twice
their pre-war total; the number of Bay Area women
employed in manufacturing leaped from 20,100 in
1940 to 73,600 in 1945. Yet it is important to recognize
that many of these women did have previous experience with paid employment in other sectors. "Wartime
employment for these women," the report noted, "was
not a venture into something new but rather part of
their continuing work experience." What was new was
the *kind* of work women were asked to do and the
fact that they had entered the workforce *en masse*,

married (fifty-seven percent of women at Marinship, for example) as well as single, rather than at discrete points in their life cycle.[54]

These fundamental changes in the place of women in the labor market proved profoundly threatening to male co-workers, husbands (and prospective husbands), and postwar reconversion planners alike. The Women's Bureau remarked on the "spectacular increase in the proportion [of women] who were employed in the manufacturing industries," from which they had been largely excluded before the war. This did not only have the social, or ideological, consequence of eroding sharply divided notions of men's and women's work, but a very practical material consequence as well: these jobs paid better than any work women had done before, and provided them with the potential means of economic independence. Women production workers in Bay Area war plants earned, on average, forty-two dollars a week, ten dollars more than they would as a waitress in the same urban area, and twice what they would earn in service sector "women's work" in a mid-western city like Wichita, Kansas. Three-quarters of the women surveyed claimed they intended to remain in the labor force, most often out of economic necessity, to provide for their own support or that of other family members.[55]

The Women's Bureau concluded that "We can neither escape the fact that women need to work nor deny them the right to a job." The report recommended the establishment of a "full employment program that will provide jobs for women as well as men" and urged upon the government "far-reaching action" on the problem of provision of adequate and affordable child care for working mothers.[56] But that was not to be. A combination of factors—returning servicemen eager for work and wives, government reconversion planning that favored men, a shrinking number of jobs, the opposition of the trade unions, and, on the part of many if hardly all women, the desire to marry, bear children, and return to the home—drove women from the work force. If one-quarter of the work force in the auto industry was female in 1945, a year later the figure had shrunk to one in twelve. In the last six months of 1945 alone, 1.32 million women were laid off from their defense jobs. At bottom, male anxiety about maintaining the role as breadwinner and fear of female economic independence, so well documented by Archibald, proved unshakeable.[57] This was an attitude encouraged even at the peak of female wartime employment in the shipyards. Even though she loved her job, *The Stinger* reported, "Pretty Margaret Beeson, one of the top women burners" claimed she would be "perfectly happy to turn over my burning torch to a man and go back to keeping house for my husband," an attitude detected by Archibald among women at Moore Dry Dock as well.[58]

"Okie, this is a Door"

The large numbers of wartime migrants from the South and Southwest, many of whom ended up working in the shipyards, fared much better in the long run, even if they too met with intense hostility at first. By 1950, 1.3 million migrants from the states of Oklahoma, Texas, Arkansas, and Missouri had made California their home over the previous four decades.[59] As Archibald points out, half of all the workers at Moore Dry Dock while she was there came from these four states. To understand the hostility encountered by these so-called "Okies" in the wartime shipyard, one had to look back to the previous decade. In the Depression years, California had been asked to accommodate a large influx of impoverished southwestern migrants driven from the heartland by collapsing farm prices, land foreclosures, and severe drought. These "Dust Bowl refugees" stretched the state's welfare system thin and competed for scarce jobs with long-time state residents. "Symbol of the state's glory in flush times," historian James Gregory points out, "interstate migration became an immediate source of concern once the economy soured."[60] As the Okies' most renowned troubadour, Woody Guthrie, sang at the time:

> If you ain't got the do re mi, boys, you ain't got the
>   do re mi,
> Why, you better go back to beautiful Texas, Oklahoma,
>   Kansas, Georgia, Tennessee.
> California is a Garden of Eden, a paradise to live in
>   or see;
> But believe it or not, you won't find it so hot
> If you ain't got the do re mi.

Prior to the wartime boom and the new opportunities it provided in the state's canneries, aircraft plants,
and shipyards, the migrants' harsh experience had
been an intensive focus not only of a folk singer like
Guthrie but also of journalists, novelists, filmmak-
ers, photographers, and sociologists, not to mention
New Deal policy makers. Immortalized in the fiction
of John Steinbeck and the photographs of Dorothea
Lange, the Okie exodus came to stand for the Depres-
sion-era California migrant experience in general.[61]
Many of the newcomers settled at first in the agricultural counties of California's Central Valley, swelling
their total population by thirty-nine percent between
1930 and 1940 at a time when they could ill-afford
such rapid expansion.[62] If after Pearl Harbor "the economic dynamic and its attendant mood had reversed
itself" in California and the state's "doors were thrown
open to all comers," the cultural stereotypes of Okies
built up during the Depression years did not dissipate
so readily.[63]

James Gregory suggests that it was the migrants'
status as impoverished farm laborers in an agricultural economy ruthlessly controlled by powerful agri-
business that stigmatized them almost to the point of
being regarded as an alien "race." If so, Archibald's
observations show that this set of prejudices was easily transferable to an industrial setting, in part because of the continuing identification of the Okies as
"backward" southerners. This was a characterization

shared by those who responded to the plight of the migrants with scorn and sympathy alike, a condescension largely avoided by Archibald, to her credit. Regarded as ignorant rural folk, unable to adjust to modern industry, city life, or a heterogeneous social environment, the southwestern migrants became the butt of many jokes and the scapegoat for many of the social tensions in overcrowded war production communities. Archibald observed that shipyard wits labeled bulkhead openings "Okie, this is a door." In a more serious vein, a clerk in Kaiser's housing office later recounted that when he asked a Kaiser worker from the rural Southwest for rent the man complained he had not been paid yet. It turned out that he had received "a piece of paper"—a paycheck, which he did not realize was money.[64]

In truth, Okie became a rather loose term in the shipyard communities of California, deployed to describe any outsider. And, unlike gender or race, it remained a mutable characteristic that could be transcended by skill, education, or personal style regardless of place of origin. Ironically, rural southern folkways were traits the Okies presumably shared with the group they themselves were most hostile to, African American migrants to the shipyards, many of whom also hailed from the rural South. In a striking encounter described in *Wartime Shipyard*, Archibald's introduction to shipyard racism came when she indelicately suggested to an Okie woman that the hostility she confronted daily on the streetcar differed little

from that she herself expressed against blacks. "But
I'm no nigger!" the object of Archibald's liberal tute-
lage cried out in horror.[65] Their experience as despised
interlopers came as a peculiar shock to Okies precisely
because, as Gregory points out, "most had always assumed that their race and heritage guaranteed a certain basic respect."[66]

they were white

This group of southern white migrants had a dramatic impact on shipyard race relations in a number
of ways. First, they brought with them racial attitudes
forged in a region steeped in a century's history of slavery, segregation, and white supremacy. Unlike whites
from other regions of the country, many of these men
and women were accustomed to daily interaction with
African Americans, but only on terms that showed
them deference and indicated their racial privilege.
In the congested, fluid, and transitory social world of
the shipyard and the surrounding communities, such
familiar racial "codes" were severely disrupted; black
workers now could defend themselves. So, for example,
the company newspaper of the Marinship shipyard,
The Stinger, reported a brawl between white and black
workers who had been gambling together, an incident
common enough that it also found its way into Himes's
fiction.[67] Moreover, the white population of the Southwest was quite homogenous compared to the rest of the
country, with little of the ethnic or religious diversity
that characterized other regions. The Kaiser shipyards'
industrial relations department reported that "the men
from the South complain more about the fact that the

shipyards employ, and they must mingle with, all races, creeds, and colors."[68] Finally, as Himes suggested and Archibald's study confirmed, an extreme phobia of interracial sexual contact, while common to most whites, especially excited the racial imagination of white southerners and provoked their violent disapproval.

Shipyard Civil Rights

Katherine Archibald proved more successful in vividly capturing the animus white workers expressed toward blacks—what she called the "depth of the hatred beneath" the "surface calm"—than she was in uncovering the actual experiences of African Americans at Moore Dry Dock. Her on-the-job, union, and social interactions remained restricted largely to other whites. Blacks had "kept to themselves for the most part," she observed. Shipyard taboos forbade any interaction between black men and white women, but she found it difficult to approach even black women. Indeed, the "only contacts of any depth or permanence" Archibald managed to establish "across the barrier of race" were with two "admittedly and openly rebellious" workers. Like other white shipyard workers, Archibald perceived some blacks' restlessness with their "place," their relentless "pushing upward" and their overt resistance to their second-class treatment. She even noticed that "groups of militant Negroes and a scattering of white collaborators" used the law to challenge union and management discrimination. But ultimately, Archibald concluded, blacks' perception of

the "futility of resistance" led them to make "little effort as a group to rebel against their segregation."[69]

If black shipyard workers didn't rebel openly, the
scope of their resistance to segregation and subordinate
status was far greater than Archibald allowed. Black
newcomers developed a reputation for aggressiveness,
reported an Alameda County deputy probation officer;
they were often "rough, very ready to fight and use
any method to win," especially to preserve their new
independence and freedom.[70] The shipyard militants'
challenges that Archibald merely alluded to were part
of a dramatic story with significant consequences for
black workers, shipyard race relations, and the stance
of organized labor toward African Americans. That
story, untold in Archibald's book, featured not only
black activists but small numbers of white leftists, re-
calcitrant white union officials and shipyard managers, the nation's leading civil rights organization (the
National Association for the Advancement of Colored
People [NAACP]), the federal government, and the
state and federal courts.

Between 1943 and 1945, thousands of African American workers in the San Francisco Bay area joined
variously named shipyard committees whose express
purpose was to challenge Jim Crow. The San Francisco Committee against Segregation and Discrimination, led by black shipyard worker, San Francisco
NAACP president, and baritone Joseph James, was the
largest, most visible, and most active of these committees, leading an ultimately successful fight at Marin-

ship Corporation in Sausalito. At Moore Dry Dock, the
Shipyard Workers Committee Against Discrimination,
led by communist Ray Thompson, launched similar
protests. Their immediate targets were the all-white
International Brotherhood of Boilermakers, Iron Ship
Builders, and Helpers of America, its segregated auxiliaries, and management compliance with the white
unionists' discriminatory practices. Demonstrations
and direct action, appeals to federal agencies, and legal suits constituted the tactics in their arsenal.

Shipyard unions, with the collaboration of shipyard
managers, were the most serious obstacle to black employment and advancement during World War II. Prior
to the war, most Bay Area industrial employment—its
shipyard industry included—was open only to white
labor; the region's small black population worked in
service or other unskilled positions. During the war,
the doors to black employment remained closed in
most industries, but shipyards were an exception.
While few blacks worked in shipbuilding prior to 1941,
by 1943 it was estimated that shipbuilding employed
as many as fifteen thousand blacks in Bay Area shipyards.[71] Company president Joseph Moore claimed
that his Moore Dry Dock was the first yard in the Bay
Area to employ African Americans. "We do not in any
way discriminate against the negro and we put additional men on as we need them should they apply," he
explained to federal officials in September 1942, add-
ing that "for many years I had negroes in my personal
employ at my home, so you see I am an advocate of

colored help." The hiring of blacks initially generated "some trouble with the unions," Moore explained, "but we insisted on their employment and they finally were able to work in the yard without much, if any, resistance from the unions."[72]

Moore was either being disingenuous or revealing his ignorance of racial conditions in his yard. Whatever the case, his explanations were misleading and subsequent events made a mockery of his claims. Black workers' access to employment was controlled wholly by shipyard unions, which had signed a master agreement with the U.S. Maritime Commission and West Coast employers in 1941 providing for the closed shop. (That is, shipyards could employ only union members.) The catch, for blacks, was that union membership was restricted to whites. Only federal pressure and the industry's voracious demand for labor, which could not be met by white workers alone, prompted the unions to permit the employment of African Americans. No sooner than entering through the shipyard gates did African Americans encounter the seemingly impenetrable walls of Jim Crow. They were initially confined to the least skilled and remunerative jobs and barred from acting in any supervisory capacity. Equally important, they were soon forced to join newly created Negro Auxiliary A-26 of Boilermakers' Local 39 as a condition of employment. That single requirement eventually sparked a shipyard civil rights movement that captured local headlines and generated considerable anxiety on the part of federal officials, even if it barely registered in Katherine Archibald's recollections.

The all-white Boilermakers' international union voted to admit blacks to all-black auxiliaries only in 1937. Auxiliary unionism could hardly even pass as separate but equal. As black activists would complain again and again, the auxiliary was a powerless entity wholly subordinate to the white union. Auxiliaries had no business agents or shop stewards (leaving the handling of grievances to white representatives); had sharp limits on their control over their own funds; could enroll no apprentices (which was crucial to training and upgrading); could not participate in the collective bargaining process (but were covered by agreements negotiated by the supervising white local); had little or no control over the distribution of jobs in the yards; and provided no transfer rights to black members seeking employment in other yards.[73] Although blacks were forced to pay full union dues, they received only half the insurance benefits of their white counterparts. Auxiliary members possessed "neither voice nor vote" in union affairs. The auxiliary was a "jimcrow 'fake' union," an "instrument of discriminatory segregation," declared Marinship activist Joseph James in 1943. Black shipyard workers initially joined the auxiliaries in good faith, James insisted, "only to find out that their money had been taken under false pretense. They found themselves in an organization in which they were segregated, disenfranchised, and dominated by people whose names they did not even know."[74] On the East Bay at Moore Dry Dock, some four thousand six hundred black employees had been forced into membership in Boilermakers' Auxiliary A-26 by the summer of 1943.[75]

Black shipyard activists' case against discriminatory treatment and auxiliary unionism was strengthened considerably by the investigations of the wartime Fair Employment Practice Committee (FEPC). To forestall a threatened march on Washington, D.C. called by black union leader A. Philip Randolph, President Franklin Roosevelt issued Executive Order 8802 in June 1941, declaring that there "shall be no discrimination in the employment of workers in defense industries or government because of race, creed, color, or national origin" and creating the FEPC to investigate complaints of discrimination in industry and trade unions.[76] On the West Coast, FEPC investigators both worked behind the scenes to persuade shipyard managers to promote black workers into more skilled positions and publicly pressured managers and unions to end their discrimination against blacks. The Boilermakers' union rejected outright the FEPC directive to cease discrimination, claiming that discrimination wasn't illegal, that the auxiliaries were not discriminatory, and that the FEPC had no legal authority to order changes in union contracts.[77]

Black shipyard workers were of no single mind on how to respond to shipyard discrimination. Some adopted the path of least resistance, joined the auxiliaries, and sought to "work from within" to improve

African Americans' position. Some officials defended
the auxiliary set-up as an effective means of allowing
blacks access to significant numbers of shipyard jobs
at good wages. Problems remained, they acknowledged, promising to "leave no stone unturned" in
efforts to better the poor living conditions of blacks
housed in company dormitories, trailers, tents and
"other unsanitary places."[78] But some rank-and-file
black workers challenged the Jim Crow set-up altogether, demanding either integration with Local 39 or
full status as a Boilermaker local. But for all their talk
of blacks' rights, they had little to show for their various efforts. Living conditions remained overcrowded
and unsanitary, black occupational advancement
proceeded at a glacial pace, and the Boilermakers appeared impervious to calls for change.[79]

Other black shipyard workers took matters directly into their own hands, refusing to pay dues to the
auxiliary unions. In Los Angeles, the San Francisco
Bay area, and Portland, rank-and-file committees
protested blacks' second-class status, launching campaigns to withhold union dues from the Auxiliaries
in 1943. Their goal, insisted members of the Marin-
ship-based San Francisco Committee against Segregation and Discrimination and the East Bay Shipyard
Workers Against Discrimination, was in no way antiunion; rather, it was to end the auxiliary system and
to achieve complete integration into the Boilermakers' locals. Refusing to budge, the white unionists pre-
cipitated a crisis by insisting that shipyard managers

enforce the closed shop contract. Since anyone who
refused to pay auxiliary dues was not an auxiliary
member and since only auxiliary or union members
could work in Bay Area shipyards, they argued, black
protesters should be discharged. In the Fall of 1943,
Boilermaker Local 6 at Marinship announced that it
would seek the discharge of four hundred and thirty
African Americans who were not in good standing with
its Auxiliary 41. In the days following a mass meeting
attended by a thousand black workers who rejected
the Boilermakers' ultimatum and reaffirmed the "no
auxiliary, come what may" strategy, the Marinship
company acceded to Boilermaker demands to pull
the time cards of roughly a hundred black Marinship
workers, effectively discharging them. An entire shift
of black shipyard workers spontaneously walked off
the job in protest. Some fifteen hundred black workers demonstrated in front of the shipyard gates. Joseph James and his San Francisco Committee against
Segregation and Discrimination secured a temporary
injunction from a federal district court restraining the
union and the company from dismissing blacks who
refused auxiliary membership.[80] But by early January
1944, the federal court concluded that it lacked jurisdiction over the case, on the grounds that no issue of
federal law was involved. The Boilermakers' renewed
insistence on the discharge of non-auxiliary blacks
was met with resistance by a state court, which issued
its own injunction blocking further action.[81]

While James pursued the Marinship workers' case

more successfully through California state courts with the assistance of the national NAACP,[82] black ship- yard activists from Los Angeles, Oakland, and Port- land agreed to cooperate in "one great, unceasing campaign for full membership in the union" in the winter of 1944. East Bay protesters, including those at Moore Dry Dock, stepped up their efforts, calling on auxiliary officials to resign, vowing to end dues pay- ments, and promoting mass applications by blacks for membership in the white union locals. By May, the Shipyard Workers Committee against Discrimination claimed that seventy-five percent of Moore's black boilermakers were withholding their dues. While this was an undoubtedly inflated figure, the efforts of black Moore employees belies Archibald's depiction of widespread passivity.[83]

The California State Supreme Court finally handed black shipyard workers a decisive legal victory in late December 1944. "An arbitrarily closed or partially closed union is incompatible with a closed shop," Chief Justice Phil S. Gibson declared. The union's "monop- oly of the supply of labor" placed it in a quasi-public position with "corresponding obligations." The Boil- ermakers' discriminatory practices, then, were "con- trary to the public policy." The result was an order to the white union either to admit blacks to membership under the "same terms and conditions applicable to non-Negroes" or to refrain from enforcing the closed shop agreement.[84] The following year, in two related cases—one of which was brought by Ray Thompson

and his shipyard committee against the Boilermakers
and Moore Dry Dock—the same court ruled decisive-
ly that the auxiliary structure itself had to be abolished.[85] In legal terms, black shipyard workers had
finally won, to a degree, their war against discriminatory unionism.

But to what effect? The *James* case ruling merely
encouraged the white Boilermakers to accord its auxiliaries independent status, not to integrate its locals.
The *Thompson* ruling, like *James*, only applied in
California. The Boilermakers officially disestablished
its auxiliaries in the state, admitting blacks to equal
membership with whites, but retained their auxiliary structure throughout the rest of the nation. In the
absence of federal law outlawing employment and
union discrimination, the legal strategy pursued by
the NAACP and the shipyard committees could only
have a limited impact. As one observer perceptively
noted, "Significant as the California Court victories
unquestionably are, we have a long way to go to get
the situation improved nationally. The Union's high
command is 'calling the shots' and they are a tough
hard boiled crowd." Only with the passage of the 1964
Civil Rights Act would segregated unions, regardless
of their status, become illegal.[86]

The timing of the black shipyard workers' victories also undercut their significance. As one of their
attorneys, Herbert Resner, concluded after the *James*
decision, "The real problem of the day . . . is the question of the future employment of Negro workers—in

fact, of all workers." The end of the war brought an end to most shipyard employment. As overall shipyard employment began its downward climb in 1944, black workers retained and even slightly improved their hold on their jobs as whites left first for other jobs, an option not available to African Americans. Such gains did not last, however. Twenty-six thousand blacks worked in Bay Area shipyards in January 1945, but by September they numbered less than twelve thousand. Local 6 of the Boilermakers' union, which represented workers in two San Francisco yards as well as at Marinship, had thirty-six thousand members, three thousand of them black, in 1944 at the time of the *James v. Marinship* case. But by 1948, while finally integrated, the union had shrunk to a mere one thousand eight hundred members, five percent of its wartime peak, with a proportional reduction of black members to one hundred fifty. By 1946, investigator Cy Record found, the number and proportion of blacks in the remaining shipyard labor force were negligible; less than three hundred remained at Moore Dry Dock, from a wartime peak of five thousand. "The result is one not entirely new in the history of the state," Record observed. A "migrant racial minority which filled an essential manpower need during a period of rapid industrial expansion" was "no longer needed or wanted." The end of the war, mass layoffs, and the closing of shipyards rendered black workers' legal victories largely moral and political ones, with little impact on the lives of the thousands of black men and women who lost their high paying shipyard jobs.[87]

Jobs may have dried up, but African Americans who had migrated to the Bay Area from the South during the war intended to stay. In 1940, there had been less than twenty thousand blacks living in the entire Bay Area. By 1949, the number had grown to one hundred twenty thousand, with forty-five thousand in Oakland alone, forty thousand across the bay in San Francisco, and in Richmond, where three hundred had resided before the war, fourteen thousand African Americans remained, even with the shutdown of the Kaiser shipyards which had initially drawn them there.[88] Many of the postwar black residents of the shipyard boomtowns of Richmond and Oakland found themselves consigned to long-term poverty, joblessness, and urban squalor. The latter city, in fact, became the breeding ground of the Black Panther Party during the 1960s, and its leader, Huey P. Newton, born in 1943, was the son of a shipyard worker who had migrated to Oakland from Louisiana during World War II.[89]

Conclusion: The Question of Social Unity

There are a number of ways to read *Wartime Shipyard* in light of the more than sixty years that have elapsed since Katherine Archibald first passed through the gates of Moore Dry Dock. Here we would like to propose two, leaving others to careful readers of Archibald's text. First, the "social disunity" Archibald found, much to her surprise, may have reflected the tensions unleashed by wartime, especially in a congested defense production area like the East Bay. "The shipyard," she wrote, "was a highly transient settlement; it was no more than a boom town which, clamorously born on one day, passed into silence on the next. Its influence as a social force was therefore limited, and its possibilities as a unifier of dissident groups were never fully realized."[90] Many local factors in Bay Area shipyards militated against the development of broad-based working-class solidarities. Sheer numbers and the intense competition for housing, transportation, and cultural space exacerbated social tensions in the shipyard communities. The overnight recomposition of the labor force, with the arrival of thousands of inexperienced workers from a myriad of backgrounds, created a heterogeneous, chaotic workplace. Extraordinarily high labor turnover throughout the war made stability virtually impossible. At the same time, government and management initiated new production methods that displaced the traditional role of skilled workers. Shipyard workers encountered few integrating institutions and the one in place, the AFL unions, did more to sharpen workplace tensions than dispel them. The significant absence of a mass-based CIO industrial union, which at least attempted to play an integrative role in defense industry communities elsewhere, highlighted these weaknesses.

Alternatively, the seemingly immovable parochialism encountered by Archibald in the shipyard may have been a more general indicator of the incredible obstacles to solidarity overcome only by the most dedicated CIO unions in the 1930s and 1940s, as well as a harbinger of things to come. Perhaps the conflicts described by Archibald can be seen as a precursor to the white working-class "backlash" against New Deal liberalism, the activist state, and multicultural cosmopolitanism, tendencies that have come to define so much of American political and historical analysis of the postwar period.[91] The key ethical foundation Archibald discovered amongst the shipyard's white working class resided narrowly in the immediate family; beyond that, generous mutual aid appeared automatic when associated with personalism, though this strict code of moral economy was undermined by the influx of new faces into the yard. Such forms of social kinship naturally drew sharp boundaries against outsiders, and easily fell prey to hierarchies of race, gender, and regional identification. The cultivated and by comparison artificial loyalties to union, class, party, state, or nation were no match for these confraternities and bundles of prejudices. The latter would persist into the postwar period, despite the best efforts of integrating institutions like the Democratic Party or the CIO. Overall, Archibald's description of the consciousness of the white working class potentially offers much to students of postwar working-class anticommunism, racism, parochialism, and conservatism.

Can broader social unities extending beyond kinship be successfully established or pursued? Archibald,

skeptical as she was, still remained hopeful. Despite
its pessimistic tone, Archibald ended her book on a
positive note, with her New Dealish faith in the possibility of "providing suitable conditions for the growth
of sociality" frayed but still intact.[92] The shipyard, in
her view, did in its common labor and social discipline at least begin to open up this prospect. But as a
temporary wartime expedient, the impact of shipyard
work dissipated rather quickly. Over half a century
later, with the New Deal order in tatters, the potential
sources of social solidarity within an increasingly diverse American working class may remain as elusive
as ever.

A Note on the Photographs

Archibald's book appears here exactly as it did in 1947,
including the four Dorothea Lange photographs accompanying the original text. Employed by the Farm
Security Administration in the 1930s, Lange had documented the Okie migration to California, and the rural poverty the in-migrants endured working in what
California social critic Carey McWilliams called "factories in the field." During the war she turned her attention to the working-class experience in the shipyard
boomtowns around San Francisco Bay. Now working
for the Office of War Information, Lange documented
the profound social upheaval and cultural transformations entailed by wartime conditions, including
the internment of Japanese Americans. Although Archibald included only four of Lange's photographs in

Wartime Shipyard, the Oakland Museum holds hundreds of her images of shipyard labor, the women and African Americans who poured into the yards, and the diverse, chaotic urban communities in Oakland and Richmond that ensued. In a very real sense this corpus of photographs still stands as the visual analogue to Archibald's work. Lange's notes and captions remain instructive. In her note on a photograph she took of the Local 513 International Brotherhood of Boilermakers, Iron Shipbuilders and Helpers hall in Richmond, Lange wrote "This was the introduction to the labor movement. Secondary unions—racial tensions . . . No Democracy." The original Lange photograph Archibald chose for the frontispiece of her book, reproduced in this edition as well, actually depicted the Kaiser shipyards rather than Moore Dry Dock. On it Lange had inscribed "All ages, races, types, skills and backgrounds. A deluge of humanity." On another photograph of workers pouring from the gates during the same Kaiser yards shift change she added, in an unusually gloomy tone Archibald might have appreciated, "Notice how people are entirely unrelated to each other."[93]

Notes

1. Chester Himes, *If He Hollers Let Him Go* (1945; rpt. New York: Thunder's Mouth Press, 2002), 15.

2. Katherine Archibald, *Wartime Shipyard: A Study in Social Disunity* (1947; rpt. Urbana: University of Illinois Press, 2006), v, 65.

3. *Fore'n Aft* 4 (April 1944), 4–5.

4. Archibald, *Wartime Shipyard*, vi.

5. We are grateful to Professor Ruth Milkman, of the University of California, Los Angeles, for gathering and passing on these tidbits of information about Archibald's background, most of it derived from her Stanford University Faculty Record, where she taught history from 1945–50. Ruth Milkman to Eric Arnesen, March 26, 1999, in authors' possession.

6. Ruth Milkman to Eric Arnesen, March 26, 1999; Katherine George to Alfred Hallowell, Dec. 7, 1951, Alfred I. Hallowell papers, American Philosophical Society (APS), Philadelphia, PA.

7. Katherine George to Alfred Hallowell, Jan. 14, 1952, Hallowell Papers, APS; Katherine George and Charles H. George, "Roman Catholic Sainthood and Social Status a Statistical and Analytical Study," *The Journal of Religion* 35 (April 1955): 85–98; Katherine George and Charles H. George, "Protestantism and Capitalism in Pre-Revolutionary England," *Church History* 27 (Dec. 1958): 351–71; Katherine George and Charles H. George, *The Protestant Mind of the English Reformation, 1570–1640* (Princeton: Princeton University Press, 1961); Manitoba Historical Society Web site, *http://www.mhs.mb.ca/docs/people/george_k.shtml*.

8. Katherine Archibald, "The Concept of Social Hierarchy in the Writings of St. Thomas Aquinas," *The Historian* 12 (1949–50): 28–54, p. 49; Katherine Archibald to Alfred Hallowell, Jan. 14, 1952, Hallowell Papers, APS.

9. For two views of this faith see Richard H. Pells, *Radical Dreams and American Visions: Culture and Social Thought in the Depression Years* (New York: Harper and Row, 1973), and Michael Denning, *The Cultural Front: The Laboring of American Culture in the Twentieth Century* (New York: Verso, 1996). Archibald, *Wartime Shipyard*, 6, 10.

10. Archibald, *Wartime Shipyard*, 10.

11. David M. Kennedy, *The American People in World War II: Freedom from Fear, Part Two* (New York: Oxford University Press, 1999), xiv, 322–23.

12. Kevin Starr, *Embattled Dreams: California in War and Peace, 1940–1950* (New York: Oxford University Press, 2002), 96.

13. Richmond population figures are from Marilynn S. Johnson, *The Second Gold Rush: Oakland and the East Bay in World War II* (Berkeley: University of California Press, 1993), 35.

14. See Dorothea Lange, *Photographing the Second Gold Rush: Dorothea Lange and the East Bay at War, 1941–1945*, with an introduction by Charles Wollenberg (Berkeley: Heyday Books, 1995).

15. David F. Selvin, *Sky Full of Storm: A Brief History of California Labor* (Berkeley: Institute of Industrial Relations, University of California, 1966), 73; Starr, *Embattled Dreams*, viii.

16. *Fore 'n Aft*, Dec. 10, 1942, quoted in Johnson, *Second Gold Rush*, 57.

17. Johnson, *Second Gold Rush*, 32; Lange, *Photographing the Second Gold Rush*, 12.

18. Archibald, *Wartime Shipyard*, 4.

19. James R. Moore, *The Story of Moore Dry Dock Company: A Picture History* (Sausalito, Cal.: Windgate Press, 1994), 6–10; Johnson, *Second Gold Rush*, 19.

20. Moore, *Story of Moore Dry Dock*, 14–18.

21. L. A. Sawyer and W. H. Mitchell, *The Liberty Ships: the History of the "Emergency" Type Cargo Ships Constructed in the United States During World War II* (Devon, Eng.: David & Charles, 1970), 11–12; Frederic C. Lane, *Ships for Victory: A History of Shipbuilding Under the U.S. Maritime Commission in World War II*, 2nd ed., with pref. by Arthur Donovan (1951; rpt. Baltimore: Johns Hopkins University Press, 2001), 10–24.

22. Moore, *Story of Moore Dry Dock*, 23–25, 212, appendix.

23. Moore, *Story of Moore Dry Dock*, 32–33.

24. Archibald, *Wartime Shipyard*, 124–25, v, 17, 41, 109, 65.

25. Two of the best accounts of these developments are Elazar Barkan, *The Retreat of Scientific Racism: Changing Con-

cepts of Race in Britain and the United States Between the World Wars (Cambridge: Cambridge University Press, 1992), 1–6; Lee D. Baker, *From Savage to Negro: Anthropology and the Construction of Race, 1896–1954* (Berkeley: University of California Press, 1998).

26. Archibald, *Wartime Shipyard*, 100, 105.

27. Archibald, *Wartime Shipyard*, 171, 170, 183.

28. Archibald, *Wartime Shipyard*, 197, 191. For various perspectives on wartime, working-class patriotism, see Gary Gerstle, "The Working Class Goes to War," in Lewis A. Erenberg and Susan E. Hirsch, eds., *The War in American Culture: Society and Consciousness During World War II* (Chicago: University of Chicago Press, 1996), 105–27; Nelson Lichtenstein, *Labor's War At Home: The CIO in World War II* (New York: Cambridge University Press, 1982; reprint, Philadelphia: Temple University Press, 2003); Nelson Lichtenstein, "The Making of the Postwar Working Class: Cultural Pluralism and Social Structure in World War II," *History Today* 51 (1988): 42–63.

29. Archibald, *Wartime Shipyard*, 61, 181, 215, 221, 236.

30. Robert D. Calkins and Walter H. Hoadley, Jr., "An Economic and Industrial Survey of The San Francisco Bay Area (Summary)" (typescript, California State Planning Board, 1942, copy in Department of Labor Library, Washington, D.C.), 19; Testimony of Charles R. Schwanenbert, April 13 and 14, 1943, in *Investigation of Congested Areas. Hearings Before a Subcommittee of the Committee on Naval Affairs*, House of Representatives, 78th Congress, First Session, Pursuant to H. Res. 30. Part 3, San Francisco, Calif., Area (Washington, D.C.: Government Printing Office, 1943), 759; Gerald D. Nash, *The American West Transformed: The Impact of the Second World War* (Lawrence: University of Kansas Press, 1985), 66–67; Henry S. Shryock, Jr., "Wartime Shifts of the Civilian Population," *Milbank Memorial Fund Quarterly* XXV, No. 3 (July 1947), 270.

31. Charles S. Johnson, et al., *The Negro War Worker in San Francisco: A Local Self-Survey* (San Francisco: YWCA, 1944),

20; Davis McEntire, "Commonwealth Club of California Study of California Population Problems, Progress Report, September 30, 1943" and Davis McEntire, "Commonwealth Club of California Study of California Population Problems Progress Report, September 30, 1943, Supplement II: The Negro Population in California (Preliminary)," in American Missionary Association Papers, *Race Relations Department, United Church Board For Homeland Ministries Archives 1943–1970* [hereafter *Homeland Ministries Archives*] (New Orleans: Amistad Research Center, Tulane University, 1979), reel 49; Johnson, *Second Gold Rush*, 83–85; Gretchen Lemke-Santangelo, *Abiding Courage: African American Migrant Women and the East Bay Community* (Chapel Hill: University of North Carolina Press, 1996), 70–72.

32. Testimony of C. E. Miller, Production Engineer, Kaiser Shipyards, and Charles R. Schwanenbert, *Investigation of Congested Areas*, 754–67; Davis McEntire, "Commonwealth Club of California Study of California Population Problems Progress Report, September 30, 1943, Supplement II: The Negro Population in California (Preliminary)," *Homeland Ministries Archives*, Reel 49; Shirley Ann Wilson Moore, *To Place Our Deeds: The African American Community in Richmond, California, 1910–1963* (Berkeley: University of California Press, 2000), 78–79; Nash, *American West Transformed*, 67.

33. Johnson, *Second Gold Rush*, 114, 121.

34. David Palmer, *Organizing the Shipyards: Union Strategy in Three Northeast Ports, 1933–1945* (Ithaca: Cornell University Press, 1998), 182.

35. Lane, *Ships for Victory*, 204–5, quote from preface, xiii.

36. Admiral Land quoted in Lane, *Ships for Victory*, 224, 238.

37. Lane, *Ships for Victory*, 204–15, quotes on 206, 215; Johnson, *Second Gold Rush*, 67–69. A paper written by Professor Daniel Letwin when he was an undergraduate at Berkeley, in 1981, "Social Change, Ideology and Social Control at the Amer-

ican Shipyards During World War Two" proved immensely helpful in emphasizing the significance of pre-fabrication to shipyard labor dynamics. We thank Professor Letwin for having the courage to share his precocious effort with us.

38. David M. Kennedy, *Freedom from Fear: America in Depression and War, 1929–1945* (New York: Oxford University Press, 2001), 779.

39. Lane, *Ships for Victory*, 237, 258.

40. Johnson, *Second Gold Rush*, 61–62, 67–76.

41. International Brotherhood of Boilermakers, Iron Shipbuilders and Helpers of America, Local 513, *Richmond: Arsenal of Democracy* (Berkeley: Tam and Gibbs Co, 1945), 33, 47, 83.

42. Sherna Berger Gluck, *Rosie the Riveter Revisited: Women, the War and Social Change* (Boston: Twayne Publishers, 1987), 8, 10, 20.

43. Sara M. Evans, *Born for Liberty: A History of Women in America* (New York: Free Press, 1989), 222–24.

44. David Kennedy suggests that "Wendy the Welder" is a more accurate term than "Rosie the Riveter" to describe women defense workers, because it better captures their high numbers in the semi-skilled trades like welding. Kennedy, *Freedom from Fear*, 779.

45. Kennedy, *Freedom from Fear*, 777–82; Lemke-Santangelo, *Abiding Courage*, 6; Moore, *To Place Our Deeds*, 57–58.

46. Booklet published by Marinship (Sausalito, 1944).

47. *Woman's Home Companion*, October 19, 1943, quoted in Gluck, *Rosie the Riveter Revisited*, 100.

48. Quoted in Ruth Milkman, "Redefining 'Women's Work': The Sexual Division of Labor in the Auto Industry During World War II," in Kathryn K. Sklar and Thomas Dublin, eds., *Women and Power in American History: A Reader*, vol. II from 1870 (Englewood Cliffs: Prentice-Hall, 1991), 209–22; quote on 213.

49. Fact Book, "Richmond Shipyards," box 287, Henry Kaiser Papers, Bancroft Library (hereafter BL), University of California, Berkeley, 30.

50. *The Stinger*, January 22, 1944, 2; "Helping the Helper-ettes," *Fore 'n Aft* 2 (December 17, 1942): 8.

51. *The Marin-er*, December 11, 1943.

52. Johnson, *Second Gold Rush*, 171–74; Evans, *Born for Liberty*, 228; John D'Emilio and Estelle B. Freedman, *Intimate Matters: A History of Sexuality in America* (New York: Harper and Row, 1988), 260; Starr, *Embattled Dreams*, 129.

53. Archibald, *Wartime Shipyard*, 38.

54. U.S. Department of Labor, *Women Workers in Ten War Production Areas and their Postwar Employment Plans*, Bulletin of the Women's Bureau No. 209 (Washington, DC: GPO, 1946), 3, 4, 36; Sherwood Hall to L. J. Scanlon, April 26, 1943, carton 1, "Industrial Advisor folder," Marinship Corporation Records, BL.

55. U.S. Department of Labor, *Women Workers*, 4, 7, 14, 19, 44.

56. U.S. Department of Labor, *Women Workers*, 23, 25.

57. Kennedy, *Freedom from Fear*, 780; Starr, *Embattled Dreams*, 157.

58. *The Stinger*, December 11, 1943.

59. James N. Gregory, *American Exodus: The Dust Bowl Migration and Okie Culture in California* (New York: Oxford University Press, 1989), 6.

60. Gregory, *American Exodus*, 79.

61. For a collaborative work of Steinbeck's newspaper articles on rural poverty accompanied by Lange's photographs see *Their Blood is Strong* (San Francisco: Simon J. Lubin Society, 1938), published prior to the appearance of Steinbeck's novel on the Dust Bowl migrants, *The Grapes of Wrath*, which shortly became a Hollywood film. *Their Blood is Strong* has been re-published as *The Harvest Gypsies: On the Road to the Grapes of Wrath* (Berkeley: Heyday Books, 1988), with an introduction by Charles Wollenberg. Lange's work at the time appeared in Dorothea Lange and Paul S. Taylor, *American Exodus: A Record of Human Erosion* (New York: Reynal and Hitchcock, 1939); many of her iconic photographs can also be found on the

Library of Congress Web site of Farm Security Administration photographs, http://memory.loc.gov/ammem/fsowhome.html. On New Deal policy and the Dust Bowl see Donald Worster, *Dust Bowl* (New York: Oxford University Press, 1982).

62. Gregory, *American Exodus*, 83.

63. Gregory, *American Exodus*, 99.

64. Archibald, *Wartime Shipyard*, 47; W. Miller Barbour, "An Exploratory Study of Socio-Economic Problems Affecting the Negro-White Relationship in Richmond, California" (Richmond: United Community Defense Services, 1952).

65. Archibald, *Wartime Shipyard*, 64.

66. Gregory, *American Exodus*, 115.

67. *The Stinger*, December 25, 1942; January 15, 1943.

68. Jean Johnson to J. C. Egan, March 9, 1943, "Industrial relations department," carton 20, Series 2, Kaiser papers, BL.

69. Archibald, *Wartime Shipyard*, 61, 86, 87, 75.

70. Quoted in Moore, *To Place Our Deeds*, 82.

71. David F. Selvin to Daniel Donovan and Judge James Wolfe, July 23, 1943, in *Records of the Committee on Fair Employment Practice 1941–1946. Field Records* [hereafter *FEPC Field Records*] (Glen Rock, N.J.: Microfilming Corporation of America, 1971), Reel 108; Albert S. Broussard, *Black San Francisco: The Struggle for Racial Equality in the West, 1900–1954* (Lawrence: University of Kansas Press, 1993), 145.

72. Joseph Moore to FEPC, September 5, 1942, *FEPC Field Records*, Reel 107; Transcript of interview conducted with Ray Thompson, November 6, 1978, Oral History Project, "Afro-Americans in San Francisco Prior to World War II," San Francisco Public Library.

73. *Report of the International President and Executive Council to the Sixteenth Consolidated Convention of the International Brotherhood of Boilermakers, Iron Ship Builders, Welders and Helpers of America, Kansas City, Mo., September 1937* (n.p. Puntom Brothers Publishing, 1937), 143, 332–33; David F. Selvin to President's Committee on Fair Employment Practice, November 2, 1943, and Memorandum, Frank S. Pestana to Harry

L. Kingman, June 10, 1944, "Re: Boilermakers," *FEPC Headquarter Records*, Reel 14; Thurgood Marshall, "Negro Status in the Boilermakers Union," *Crisis* (March 1944), 77–78.

74. Joseph James, "Against the Setting Up of Auxiliary Unions for Negroes (Specifically, Boilermakers' Local #6)," June 11, 1943, *FEPC Field Records*, Reel 108; Joseph James, "Report on Aux. Situation with Reference to Int. Brotherhood of Boilermakers, Local #6, and Negro Workers of Marinship Corp., Bethlehem, & Western Pipe and Steel," December 21, 1943, *FEPC Headquarter Records*, Reel 14; William H. Harris, "Federal Intervention in Union Discrimination: FEPC and West Coast Shipyards During World War II," *Labor History* 22, No. 3 (Summer 1981), 327–28.

75. Office Memorandum, Daniel R. Donovan to George M. Johnson, August 5, 1943, "Subject: Conferences at San Francisco," *FEPC Headquarter Records*, Reel 15.

76. On the March on Washington Movement and the origins of the FEPC, see: Eric Arnesen, *Brotherhoods of Color: Black Railroad Workers and the Struggle for Equality* (Cambridge: Harvard University Press, 2001); Paula F. Pfeffer, *A. Philip Randolph, Pioneer of the Civil Rights Movement* (Baton Rouge: Louisiana State University Press, 1990), 46–55; Merl E. Reed, *Seedtime for the Modern Civil Rights Movement: The President's Committee on Fair Employment Practice, 1941–1946* (Baton Rouge: Louisiana State University Press, 1991); Charles D. Chamberlain, *Victory at Home: Manpower and Race in the American South during World War II* (Athens: University of Georgia Press, 2003).

77. "New U.S. Order is Hailed; Marinship Case in Balance," *People's World*, December 15, 1943; "Weekly Report . . . April 1, 1944," Kingman to Maslow, April 3, 1944, carton 3, folder 27, Harry Lees Kingman, Correspondence and Papers, 1922–75 (hereafter Kingman Papers), BL; Office Memorandum, Frank D. Reeves to George M. Johnson, January 24, 1944, "Subject: Legal Issues Raised by the Boilermakers Union," *FEPC Headquarter Records*, Reel 15.

78. Leon Washington, Jr., "War Work Boom But Living Conditions Wretched Reporter Finds on Tour of California," Houston *Negro Labor News*, January 20, 1943.

79. "Fight for Integration in Boilermakers' Union," *Kansas City Call*, February 4, 1944; "Boilermakers Keep Auxiliary Set-Up," *Pittsburgh Courier*, February 19, 1944; Office Memorandum, Daniel R. Donovan to George M. Johnson, "Subject: Conferences at San Francisco," August 5, 1943, *FEPC Headquarter Records*, Reel 15; Office Memorandum, Frank D. Reeves to George M. Johnson, February 24, 1944, "Subject: Action of the Seventeenth Consolidate Convention of the IBBMISB&H of A," *FEPC Headquarter Records*, Reel 14; Report on Auxiliary Situation (San Francisco) as of March 24th, 1944, *NAACP Papers, Part 13, Series C*, Reel 1.

80. James, "Report on Aux. Situation . . .," December 21, 1943, *FEPC Headquarter Records*, Reel 14; "Weekly Report for the Week Ending Saturday, November 20, 1943," Harry Kingman to Will Maslow, November 22, 1943, "Weekly Report for the Week Ending Saturday, November 27, 1943," Kingman to Maslow, November 29, 1943, "Weekly Report," Kingman to Maslow, December 6, 1943, "Weekly Report," Kingman to Maslow, December 14, 1943," carton 2, folder 25, Kingman Papers, BL; "On the Scene of Walkout at Marinship—11/27/43," *Homeland Ministries Archives*, Reel 49; "Non-Union Workers May Regain Jobs," *Daily Californian*, November 29, 1943; "Ross Wires Union to Halt Dismissals," *Pittsburgh Courier*, December 4, 1943; Charles Wollenberg, *"James v. Marinship:* Trouble on the New Black Frontier," in Daniel Cornford, ed., *Working People of California* (Berkeley: University of California Press, 1995), 166–70.

81. Joseph James, "The Marinship Case During the Month of January, 1944," *FEPC Headquarter Records*, Reel 14; "Jim Crow Union Battle is Reopened," *San Francisco Chronicle*, January 4, 1944; "Weekly Report . . . January 15, 1944," Kingman to Maslow, January 17, 1944, "Weekly Report . . . January 22, 1944, Kingman to Maslow, January 24, 1944," and "Weekly

Report, February 19, 1944," Kingman to Maslow, February 21, 1944, carton 2, folder 26, Kingman Papers, BL.

82. "Court Backs Negro Ship Workers," *New York Times*, February 18, 1944.

83. Report on Auxiliary Situation (San Francisco) as of March 24th, 1944, *Papers of the NAACP, Part 13, Series C*, Reel 1; Ray Stewart, Vice Chairman, Shipyard Workers Committee Against Discrimination to War Labor Board, May 19, 1944, and Kingman to George M. Johnson, May 21, 1944, *FEPC Headquarter Records*, Reel 14.

84. *Joseph James et. al. v. Marinship Corporation, International Brotherhood of Boilermakers, Iron Shipbuilders and Helpers of America, et. al.*, 9 Labor Cases 67,161; NAACP Press Release, "California Supreme Court Outlaws Jim Crow Auxiliary Unions," January 4, 1945, *Papers of the NAACP, Part 13, Series C*, Reel 1; "Court Bids Union Take in Negroes," *New York Times*, January 3, 1945.

85. *Raymond F. Thompson etc. et al., Appellants, v. Moore Drydock Company et al.* (27 A.C. January 1946); "AF of L Unit Denied Right to Bar Race," *Pittsburgh Courier*, February 9, 1946.

86. International Brotherhood of Boilermakers, April 23, 1946, Resolution; "Memorandum to Mr. Harrington From Thurgood Marshall: For Press Release, May 22, 1946," George M. Johnson to Thurgood Marshall, June 12, 1946, and Herbert Resner to Thurgood Marshall, May 15, 1945, *Papers of the NAACP, Part 13, Series C*, Reel 1. On the limits of the federal courts in rectifying discrimination, see Arnesen, *Brotherhoods of Color*, 203–29.

87. Herbert Resner to Thurgood Marshall, April 4, 1945, *Papers of the NAACP, Part 13, Series C*, Reel 1; Wollenberg, *"James v. Marinship,"* 174; Cy W. Record, "Characteristics of Some Unemployed Negro Shipyard Workers in Richmond" (typescript, Intergovernmental Studies Library, University of California at Berkeley, 1947); Davis McEntire and Julia R. Tarnopol, "Postwar Status of Negro Workers in San Francisco Area," *Monthly*

Labor Review 70, No. 6 (June 1950), 612–17; Cy W. Record, "The Negro-White Issue in California," *Labor and Nation* IV, No. 3 (May-June 1948), 25–27; Cy W. Record, "Willie Stokes at the Golden Gate," *Crisis* 56 (June 1949): 175–79, 187.

88. Record, "Willie Stokes at the Golden Gate," 175–76, 187; Moore, *To Place Our Deeds*, 95–97.

89. Robert O. Self, *American Babylon: Race, Power, and the Struggle for the Postwar City in California* (Princeton: Princeton University Press, 2003); Judson L. Jeffries, *Huey P. Newton: The Radical Theorist* (Jackson: University Press of Mississippi, 2002), xix-xxi.

90. Archibald, *Wartime Shipyard*, 236.

91. A brief sampling includes Thomas J. Sugrue, *The Origins of the Urban Crisis: Race and Inequality in Postwar Detroit* (Princeton: Princeton University Press, 1996); Kenneth D. Durr, *Behind the Backlash: White Working-Class Politics in Baltimore* (Chapel Hill: University of North Carolina Press, 2003); Dan T. Carter, *From George Wallace to Newt Gingrich: Race in the Conservative Counterrevolution, 1963–1994* (Baton Rouge: Louisiana State University Press, 1990); Thomas Byrne Edsall and Mary D. Edsall, *Chain Reaction: The Impact of Race, Rights and Taxes on American Politics* (New York: Norton, 1991); Christopher Lasch, *The True and Only Heaven: Progress and Its Critics* (New York: Norton, 1991); Thomas Frank, *What's the Matter With Kansas? How Conservatives Won the Heart of America* (New York: Metropolitan Books, 2004). For an alternative explanation see Judith Stein, *Running Steel, Running America: Race, Economic Policy, and the Decline of Liberalism* (Chapel Hill: University of North Carolina Press, 1998).

92. Archibald, *Wartime Shipyard*, 235.

93. Lange, *Photographing the Second Gold Rush*, 10–11, 18–19; Dorothea Lange collection, notes for file 42097, notes for file 42084, Oakland Museum of California, Oakland, California.

FURTHER READING

❧ WE THOUGHT it would be useful to call direct attention to some of the more important and readily accessible material cited above in the notes to our introduction. Faculty looking for works to consult or assign and students working on paper topics or interested in learning more about the milieu in which Archibald researched *Wartime Shipyard* can begin with some of the following works.

The most thorough recent survey of American history during the war years is David M. Kennedy, *The American People in World War II: Freedom from Fear, Part Two* (New York, 1999); chapter 8, "The Cauldron of the Home Front," pp. 321–72, is especially relevant. For a general history of the social, economic, and cultural impact of World War II on California specifically, the best introduction is Kevin Starr's breezy yet inclusive *Embattled Dreams: California in War and Peace, 1940–1950* (New York, 2002), the sixth volume in his massive "Americans and the California Dream" series. For a more focused and scholarly study of the transformations of California's major urban areas, including those in the Bay Area, see Roger Lotchin, *The Bad City in the Good War: San Francisco, Los Angeles, Oakland, and San Diego* (Bloomington, 2003). And for a comprehensive social history of the East Bay in this same period, with a strong emphasis on shipyard labor, students and instructors should consult Marilynn

S. Johnson, *The Second Gold Rush: Oakland and the East Bay in World War II* (Berkeley, 1993). The story of photographer Dorothea Lange's visual documentation of this same history can be found in *Photographing the Second Gold Rush: Dorothea Lange and the East Bay at War, 1941–1945* (Berkeley, 1995), with an excellent introduction by local historian Charles Wollenberg, who also authored a study of the Bay Area shipyard in which black activist Joseph James was employed, *Marinship at War: Shipbuilding and Social Change in Wartime Sausalito* (Berkeley, 1990). A very useful collection of historical essays on various aspects of wartime life in California, especially the impact of the war on the state's minority communities, is Roger Lotchin, ed., *The Way We Really Were: The Golden State in the Second Great War* (Urbana, 2000).

Modern historians of the Bay Area and California have produced local studies of many of the groups discussed in Archibald's book. Some of the best include Shirley Ann Moore's history of the black population in Richmond (home of the Kaiser shipyards), *To Place Our Deeds: The African American Community in Richmond, California, 1910–1963* (Berkeley, 2000), James N. Gregory's chronicle of the Okie migration, *American Exodus: The Dust Bowl Migration and Okie Culture in California* (New York, 1989), and, on California labor, though not confined to the World War II era, the essays collected in Daniel Cornford, ed., *Working People of California* (Berkeley, 1995). Cornford's book can be supplemented by older brief but sweeping surveys of the state's labor history by journalist David F. Selvin, most notably his *Sky Full of Storm: A Brief History of California Labor* (Berkeley, 1966) or *A Place in the Sun: A History of California Labor* (San Francisco, 1981). Still an outstanding source on the reorganization of production and the dynamics of wartime shipyard labor, over fifty years after its initial publication, is Frederic C. Lane, *Ships for Victory: A History of Shipbuilding Under the U.S. Maritime Commission in World War II*, 2nd ed. (1951; rpt. Baltimore, 2001), chapters 7–9 and 13. Gretchen Lemke-Santangelo's *Abiding Courage: African American Migrant Women and the East Bay Community* (Chapel Hill, 1996) specifically addresses the wartime experience of black women, many of them from the South, who traveled to the Bay Area to find jobs in defense industries like shipbuilding. Although not limited to California history, Daniel A. Cornford and Sally M. Miller, eds., *American Labor in the Era of World War II* (Westport, Conn., 1995) includes essays by Marilynn Johnson, Shirley Ann Moore, and Gretchen Lemke-Santangelo, drawn from their book-length works cited above, in addition to four other chapters on California labor during the war. Robert O. Self's *American Babylon: Race, Power, and the Struggle for the Postwar City in California* (Princeton, 2003), explores the history of Oakland's African American population from the end of the war through the 1960s, and can be consulted in conjunction with sociologist Chris Rhomberg's *No There There: Race, Class, and Political Community in Oakland* (Berkeley, 2004), a sweeping analysis of the city's urban politics in the twentieth century. Of course, nearly all of the work of Carey McWilliams remains indispensable for anyone interested in the long history of class and ethnic tensions in California; see especially his classic *Factories in the Field: The Story of Migratory Farm Labor in California* (1939; rpt. Berkeley, 2000); *California: The Great Exception* (1949; rpt. Berkeley, 1999); and *Prejudice: Japanese-Americans, Symbols of Racial Intolerance* (Boston, 1944), regrettably still out of print.

Unfortunately, there is no single book-length study of the working lives of California's women wartime shipyard workers, but those interested in pursuing this topic can read Sherna Berger Gluck's oral history, *Rosie the Riveter Revisited: Women, the War and Social Change* (Boston, 1987), view the excellent 1980 documentary film by Connie Field, "The Life and Times of Rosie the Riveter," and visit the Richmond-based website on "Rosie," *www.rosietheriveter.org*. Studies of women shipyard workers elsewhere in the country include Amy Kesselman, *Fleeting Opportunities: Women Shipyard Workers in Portland and Vancouver during World War II and Reconversion* (Albany, 1990) and Mary Martha Thomas, *Riveting and Rationing in Dixie: Alabama Women and the Second World War* (Tuscaloosa, 1987). Ruth Milkman's book, *Gender at Work: The Dynamics of Job Segregation by Sex during World War II* (Urbana, 1987), looks closely at women working in wartime automobile, aviation and electrical parts plants, and a chapter in Emily Yellin, *Our Mothers' War: American Women at Home and at the Front During World War II* (New York, 2005), offers a useful recent survey of women's wartime work.

Three different accounts of the national legal ramifications of the black challenge to workplace discrimination during the war, with an emphasis on the role of the Boilermakers' Union in maintaining racial barriers in shipyard work, are Merl A. Reed, *Seedtime for the Modern Civil Rights Movement: The President's Committee on Fair Employment Practice, 1941–1946* (Baton Rouge, 1991), Herbert Hill, *Black Labor and the American Legal System: Race, Work, and the Law* (Madison, 1985), 173–382, and especially germane to the events discussed in our introduction, Charles Wollenberg, *"James v. Marinship:* Trouble on the New Black Frontier,*"* in Cornford, ed, *Working People of California,* 159–79. For an article examining the explosive confluence of race and sex in the wartime workplace see Eileen Boris, *"'*You Wouldn't Want One of 'Em Dancing With your Wife': Racialized Bodies on the Job in World War II,*"* *American Quarterly* 50 (March 1998): 77–108. Powerful fictional treatments of the same dynamic, both profitably read in conjunction with *Wartime Shipyard* are Chester Himes, *If He Hollers Let Him Go* (1945; rpt. New York, 2002), set in the Los Angeles area, and Alexander Saxton, *Bright Web in the Darkness* (New York, 1958), which focuses on the East Bay, republished in 1997 by the University of California Press. Instructors might consider assigning papers asking students to use Archibald's book, one of these two novels, published and on-line oral histories, and the film "The Life and Times of Rosie the Riveter" to explore the implications of racial and gender conflicts in the wartime work place.

PREFACE TO THE ORIGINAL

❦ As these pages *go to press, the war, which was the temporal occasion for their writing, is almost two years distant. The shipyard boom town, their spatial setting, is likewise gone, and the slap-slap of estuary water can be clearly heard in the silence that envelops slips and dry docks once clamorously busy.*

But the subject which occupies this study is only incidentally a period past and a situation vanished. Its primary concern is not a wartime shipyard, but the people who during a war worked in a shipyard, and the attitudes they cherished. More specifically, it seeks to analyze these people and their attitudes in reference to the problem of social disunity. Both the war and the shipyard thus become merely the narrow and temporary context for discussion of a problem which extends in space over all the world and in time throughout human history.

The method of this analysis inevitably proceeds from fairly particular experiences to fairly general applications and conclusions. Such intellectual venturing, however, arises quite naturally from the facts which are its base. The wartime shipyard drew within its boundaries an extraordinarily large and representative sampling of the working masses of America. Furthermore, it constrained these workers to endure intimacies of contact which seemed almost to have been consciously intended to stimulate the fundamental mechanisms of disunity. The hatreds and suspicions which divide group from group were here displayed in wonderful detail and under brilliant light. No especial recklessness of mind was implied, therefore, in the expansion of ship-yard observations into a larger sphere of investigation and debate.

Today in peace, more obviously than in war, the future of man depends on the emergence and the main-tenance of inclusive social unities. Indeed, in this atomic age with complete catastrophe a present threat, the need grows ever more imperative for any knowledge which will illuminate the areas of social strain and make possible a strengthening of the communal struc-ture. It is not in the service of a minor or merely aca-demic issue then that this study makes its stand, but rather as a contribution to the understanding of a prob-lem with which the living hopes and fears of men are intimately entangled. To the degree to which the story told here fulfills this purpose it remains, like the prob-lem with which it deals, contemporary.

K. A.

Palo Alto, California
December 5, 1946

WARTIME SHIPYARD

THE SHIPYARD

❧ THE SHIPYARD of the war years was a boom town of huddled buildings and long-necked cranes that rose overnight from the mud flats of a bay or river frontage. Through its gates passed twenty or thirty or forty thousand men and women every twenty-four hours. During most of their working time, as they moved singly or in scattered groups from one task to another, they were overshadowed and lost in the mass of what they built and the tools with which they built it. But when, with the rhythmic certainty of sunrise and sunset, the change-of-shift hours came, the real magnitude of the human force impounded behind the gates and miles-long fences became apparent. The inward flow coming on shift spilled into the yard reservoir, and filled it; and the homegoing surge poured forth, at first confined by the narrow funnel of the gates, then spreading out over the wide plain of the surrounding community and dwindling into a multitude of trickling streams. Three times a day, one society with common tasks and purposes was formed at the shipyard entrance while another emerged; but the unity of shipyard society was no greater than that of a boom town which collapses when the vein runs out. The only bond that held together its components, who were drawn from a continent of space and a whole nation of differing social backgrounds, was the chance and temporary pressure of a wartime need. Ships had to be built.

For months after December 7, 1941, the shipyards of the West Coast were ravenous for men, and they used effective propaganda to lure workers from all corners of the land. The bait was good: the wages offered were high, and the climate was a well-advertised bonus. Moreover, shipbuilding was an industry essential to the war effort, and many draft-age men were not unwilling to enlist in the industrial service. From farms where the lure of the city was legend, from small businesses dying on the vine, from offices where the draft blew icily down white collars, from lunchrooms that paid too little, from kitchen drudgery that had seemed inescapable, from professions that now in the excitement of wartime seemed boresome—from all these, and many other places and conditions, multitudes came to the shipyards. And the shipyards absorbed them all. Color, age, sex, soundness of limb did not matter; whoever could walk or lift a welder's stinger was welcomed.

The variety of persons engaged in the actual hand-dirtying work of the yards was not quite infinite, of course. In terms of the social levels which were tapped there was a fairly consistent ceiling. The businessman, the man of wealth or influence, who desired to serve in an essential industry during the war period, seldom got farther inside the gates than the front office; and the

occasional patriotic clubwoman or socialite who ventured to put on a welder's hood soon took it off and departed from the filth and clamor. For the most part,
those who wore overalls in the shipyard had worn them
before on the farm or in the factory, or at best, as office
clerk or small-time salesman, had known the frayed
white collar. The shipyard women were the wives and
daughters of such men. The great expansion in the social
areas reached by shipyard demands for manpower consisted in the lowering of the floor and the drawing in
of the masses of the unskilled who were customarily
ignored by peacetime industry. To the unlettered and
untaught, the drifters and the failures, farmers and
farm workers scrabbling on the borderline of subsistence, Negroes cramped in opportunity by prejudice,
and women who in peacetime constituted only a reserve
for casual and poorly paid work—to the entire group
of the underprivileged, the exploited, and the unorgan-
ized the outburst of shipyard activity gave a chance to
participate in the skilled trades and to partake of their
rewards. Within these limits the shipyard world was
extraordinarily mixed, and brought together in a working relationship many groups which ordinarily were
separated by geographical and social barriers.

The differences that divide the people of the United
States into regional groups and hierarchical layers were
painfully juxtaposed in the shipyard settlement. It was

a society larger, more varied, and more restless than that to which most of its components were accustomed; a society so irregular, indeed, as to confound every local tradition of proper social relationships. The white workers were compelled to associate with Negroes on terms of intimacy—an intimacy which to the southern whites, at least, was unusual and repugnant. Craftsmen reared in the exacting traditions of their trade were obliged to extract what service they could from the un-skilled farm boy and, more shocking still, from women who smelled of the kitchen and the beauty parlor. And the very nature of the shipyards and the work that was done there were a continual reminder of the wartime demand for subordination of cherished localisms to larger social unities. The reminder might be resisted, but it could not be ignored.

The shipyard where I went to work in the late summer of 1942—of the Moore Dry Dock Company, Oakland, California—was representative of them all. Moore Dry Dock was an established industry which for nearly half a century had been carrying on some kind of shipbuilding and repair; it had seen one war boom come and go, and was now entering upon a sec-ond period of expansion which was to increase its per-sonnel to the thirty-five thousand mark, add an entire new section to the plant (the West as distinguished from the old East Yard), and finally extend the equipment of modern ship construction and repair over a square mile of what had once been cattail-cluttered slough. It was an institution with some roots in the past; but the fertilization with government contracts produced here a wartime bloom that no old-timer would ever have recognized.

Fences and guarded gates, cranes and huddled buildings, men and women of many backgrounds, and tensions generated by many conflicting insularities—these, during my first weeks at the yard, were so bewildering that in adapting myself I could not intelligently observe others as they too were affected by the new environment. For the first time in my adult life, moreover, I was brought actually into contact with the working masses of America, the vast group to which I had long since given my theoretical sympathies. I had come to the shipyards as an academician and a liberal whose experience with the social problems of America had been gained in libraries and the occasional concourse of like-thinking minds. My conclusions about the miseries of man, his insufficiencies and his conflicts, were orthodox; my solutions were simple, and, like others of my persuasion, I was confident of possessing truth in all its possible infallibility and brilliance. When I stepped from the world of theory into the wider world of fact, it was as if I had suddenly passed from the dimness of a monastic cell into the glare of an outdoor noon; and for a while, blinking and astonished, I could not distinguish the shapes of what I saw.

As I became adjusted to my new environment, I discovered that the magnitude of fact dwarfed my simple preconceptions. Where logic and liberal theory had promised some sense of unity among the shipyard workers, derived from their common interests and common status, I found in actuality differences and gaps—social abysses so deep that the possibility of spanning them never occurred, apparently, to right-minded people reared after a righteous custom. I found intolerance of slight linguistic and cultural differences so great that the ghosts of feudal snobbery seemed to have come alive. I found insularities so narrow as scarcely to be believed. Even among these people, for whose sake the liberal had contrived his dream of equalitarianism, I found that the lesser inequalities were cherished, and the weaker suppressed by the less weak. Where I had confidently expected unity of purpose and of action, I found only antagonism and turmoil.

THE PROBLEM OF DISUNITY

❧ SOCIAL DISUNITY is as wide as the world and as deep as human history. Its larger consequences in war and revolution have been a chief source of the moralist's sorrow and the cynic's acrid scorn. Indeed, some students, observing the centrifugal forces continually at work within society, have defined the social bond as an artificial union of disparate elements which resist all constraint. Historical manifestations of social disunity have been twofold: vertical conflict has existed between competing classes, hierarchically arranged within a given social unit; and horizontal conflict has existed between separate groups which, while standing on a plain of relative equality, have marked their borderlines with fire and blood. In the course of centuries of restless struggle, sectors of the conflict have quieted in a partial settlement of their differences; the processes of democracy have begun to solve the difficulties arising from class distinctions, and expansion of the state has relieved several of the severest tensions of intergroup antagonism. But the problem of disunity as a whole still finds its unequivocal solution only in the realm of Utopian fancy and the uninhibited dream.

A unique poignancy attaches to the problem of social disunity as it exists in the American scene. For three centuries America gladly played host to the discontented and oppressed: there were horizons to be crossed, countless tasks in cities, forests, and mines awaited doing, and America asked few questions of those who came. The vision arose of this land as the crucible into which many elements of an old world could be melted, to emerge at last an alloy in one piece and of one quality. The conviction was widespread that the difference between classes, the ancient burden of those who came to America, would prove no lengthy problem to the wonderful metallurgy of the melting pot.

Confidence has since been lessened. To begin with, the economic basis of American civilization has changed. The far horizons are no more; the unexploited resources have dwindled, and as a consequence the children's children of immigrants have chosen to exclude the immigrant lest the nation's wealth be subjected to further sharing. More than two decades have passed since the door was shut on Europe and Asia—time enough for America's continuities, its established boundaries and common traditions, to exert uninterrupted force upon the task of integrating a heterogeneous people; but that the crucible has failed to work its miracles has become more obvious, the deeper observers have probed into the presumed unity of American life. With the shock and horror of those who, after the dust storms, looked about and found eroded the once-level plains of the

Southwest, the students of American society have awakened to find their dream plains of unity gashed by canyons which time serves only to deepen.

As the approach of World War II reëmphasized America's disunities, they became a subject of increasing concern; for war, of course, demands subordination of lesser disputes to the service of the common battle. In the frantic search for a unity of thought and action America discovered the depth of its social canyons. Regional antagonisms, race riots, class distinctions—these physical facts rudely disturbed the dream of One America. Facts they are, the facts of ever more devastating wars, and of continual cold hostilities between peoples which even more effectively have obscured the vision of a united world. A thousand facts, more resistant than stone, stand between the theorist and the dearest hope he cherishes of a society which from one viewpoint is single and indivisible and from another is exactly as diverse as the number of personalities composing it.

To the facts which are the basis of social disunity, to the deeds and attitudes which produce and maintain it, the academic liberal whose anxieties are centered in society and its fate must somehow find his way. With a sense of urgency befitting the time—for as the techniques of mass destruction grow more effective, the menace of disunity increases—he must pursue his search for the facts which are significant to analysis, explanation, and solution of the problem. These facts, moreover, are not primarily to be found in the writings of social theorists and philosophers, nor in the pronouncements of statesmen and the leaders of the mass, where heretofore they have commonly been sought, but rather in the obscure depths of society, in the back streets of cities and of small towns of the hinterland, and in the ordinary relationships of ordinary folk. For the tower of a structure is no more secure than the foundation on which it rests, and at the point of trial the ideals of world unity are no more substantial than the attitudes of the common people.

By many liberals, much responsibility for advance toward the equalitarian and universalistic goal has been credited to the common people. Tracing the connection between the disunities of society and the predatory interests of a ruling class, liberals have tended to assume that with the removal of the pernicious influences of power and of the insecurities which are the corollaries of a system of predation, group antagonism and oppression of minorities will at least be greatly ameliorated. The masses, they argue, are disunited against their own judgment and inclination, and inevitably will rediscover their rightful unity, first as a class and eventually in the vast harmony of an equalitarian society.

The logic of liberal reasoning is indisputable since

the masses of men are always in some manner the victims and not the beneficiaries of the conflicts of their societies, and since they all suffer to some degree the burdens of subservience and discrimination which are the classical stigmata of the minority. Were knowledge and rationality the guiding principles of social change, the masses of men, who all pay the penalties of an inequalitarian society, would certainly be the proper repository of liberal faith. But unfortunately, in writing their books and in issuing their advice, liberal thinkers have too often consulted the logic rather than the actualities of the situation. Theorizing about the masses, they have seldom dealt with them on the level of mutual understanding or effective action. In their ignorance of human association they have oversimplified the problem of social disunity, and have aided in its correct interpretation and solution far less than they might have done.

In reference to the problem of social disunity and the search for a solution the shipyard community assumes its particular significance, for it contained in small spatial and temporal compass the components of the American scene most suitable to a study of group relationships and adjustments. Like all boom towns, the shipyard represented the melting pot in its most dramatic function. Difference was flung against difference, localism against localism, and prejudice against prejudice with regard for nothing but the urgency of the immediate wartime task. Through the shipyard "Ellis Island" thronged the inhabitants of America's various geographical and social regions, to be subjected to a fleeting but intense process of unification. During his active employment the shipyard worker was constrained, ultimately by his own self-interest, to accept whatever status and associates his job offered. The social reach of the shipyard was, furthermore, so extensive as to include a sampling from almost every region of America and from most of the groups which make up the nation's working population. Men of many crafts, races, and backgrounds were congregated there during wartime; hence, reactions and attitudes which occurred in the shipyard might be assumed to prevail elsewhere. The shipyard, then, was a laboratory for the student of society.

participant observer I make no claim to having achieved the objectivity which this comparison suggests, since during my shipyard experience I was not only an observer of a reaction and its end products, but also and perhaps primarily a reagent, too intimately concerned ever to seize and hold a place of complete detachment. But my very preoccupation entailed certain compensating advantages; I was enabled thereby to fulfill at least one of the criteria of accurate observation, for I came close to my subject—close enough to be a part of it.

My technique of investigation was simple and was suggested by my jobs. As storekeeper on the hulls, expediter of materials, or warehouse clerk, I had to talk a great deal with many and various co-workers. I talked, and learned also to listen. After a period of difficult adjustment I acquired the shipyard language and idiom. I discovered how to ask questions without arousing hostility or obtaining answers that were stilted, shaped to suit the moment, and distorting of real attitude. I became proficient in selective eavesdropping. And then in idle minutes I copied into a notebook the significant comments and conversations which I had gathered, preserving as much of the original freshness and flavor as my ear was able to retain. The method had no formality. Even though many hundred items were collected in my notebook, no charts and tables could ever come from it. But in view of my purposes and interests the procedure that I followed seemed to me most suitable. What I sought and what I obtained was depth rather than breadth of observation. I came to know a few things well.

This account of two years of experience and observation is perhaps best described as a tale of pilgrimage. It is the story of one academic liberal who went forth into the realm of social fact with the usual luggage of preconception and, in the course of the journey, found that one piece after another had to be discarded or lightened. It is a tale, however, not so much of disillusion—though sloughs of despond were frequent along the way—as of revelation. For, properly viewed, any knowledge, even that which is painfully destructive of cherished illusion, is revelation. And in knowledge alone, true, sound, and uncontaminated with false sentiment, all fruitful plans for the reconstruction of society and the regeneration of man can begin.

WOMEN IN THE SHIPYARD

✢ IN SHIPYARD relationships, the difficulty of which I was earliest aware pertained neither to scorn of a people nor to affirmation of the fixed and wholesale inferiority of a class. I was first aroused from my vision of equalitarianism by the need to defend, against the resentment of the masculine majority, my personal right as a woman to be where I had chosen to come. The background of such resentment is, of course, well known and well documented, but its manifestations in the shipyard were so strong as to force my consideration of it as a personal problem.

Before the war, most heavy industries, especially ship construction, had provided one of the few occupational areas upon which the pressure of feminism had been exerted in vain. They were protected by the comfortable conviction that the work was so complex and arduous as to remain forever beyond the weaker grasp of womankind. And then December 7th struck, and the needs of war became paramount over all conviction. A typical pattern was established at Moore Dry Dock. Here, women were beginning to intrude into the actual work of construction by the late spring of 1942, first as welders, then as laborers and electricians, and finally, a growing stream, into almost all the crafts of shipbuilding.

[15]

Men were amazed. Groups would gather about a lone girl welder and stare at her and her handiwork as at a circus freak. For their work at welding plates, the women were put at first in open sheds "where everybody could keep an eye on them." Not until the fall were they permitted on the hulls as workers, and even then they were stationed only on the top decks. But as astonishment lessened and an occasional whistle took the place of the gawking stare, the limitations upon the usefulness of women were more and more withdrawn, and by the spring of 1943 women had obviously become a stable and inevitable factor in the economy of the wartime shipyard. By summer, the period of peak employment, women comprised approximately twenty per cent of the total working force of more than thirty-five thousand, and that percentage was maintained into the late months of 1944.

In their ordinary relationships with women workers most of the men were courteous and even gallant. As the women infiltrated the hulls and the remoter shacks of the yard, the men amiably removed their galleries of nudes and pornography from the walls and retired them to the gloom of the tool box. In deference to the presence of "ladies," manners were improved, faces were shaved more often, and language was toned down. The taboo against improprieties of speech within earshot of women was so extreme as to be amusing, particularly since the women themselves frequently gave audible proof that the forbidden words were neither unfamiliar nor disturbing to them. Yet I have often seen men who wanted to use strong language, and with good excuse for it, flush with sudden embarrassment and drop their voices to a mutter on becoming conscious of a feminine audience. In the lunchtime companionship of men and women workers and in the casual chat at any leisure moment, in all that pertained to familiar social contacts, even amid the unfamiliar surroundings of the shipyards, the men preserved almost intact the pattern of behavior which they practiced at home: the respect for the decent wife and the good mother, the circumspect friendliness with the sister, and even the protective affection for the inexperienced daughter of the family. But underneath the formality and politeness a half-concealed resentment still persisted, not against women as women, but against them as rivals of men in a man's world. In the bull session, the passing insult, and the occasional public expression of opinion the coals of this antagonism would leap to flame.

In large part, however, masculine antagonism constituted a vague and emotion-charged atmosphere rather than any well-defined and rational position. It was somewhat deviously manifested in the emphasis in shipyard talk and behavior upon the sexual role of women, proper enough in the traditional locale of the home

and the bordello but both improper and dangerous
when intermixed with the serious work of the world.
Here, too, was something of primitive man's anxiety
lest a woman of the tribe might chance to come in contact with his weapons, his tools, or his sacred objects
and spoil their potency by her touch or glance. In the
modern as in the primitive environment, elaborate
precautions were employed to control encroachments.
Whatever the degree of adjustment, whatever the outward appearance of harmony, the ancient doctrine was
never wholly abandoned—that the real and only power
of women was the power of sex and that their sole possible contribution to the field of maculine endeavor was
one of negative distraction and disturbance rather than
positive aid.   *wow*

Sex attitudes made up the tangled background of the
male worker's point of view. Sex was his great avoca-
tional interest. Whether bounded by the proprieties of
marriage or unconstrained in the reaches of bachelor
fancy, it was the spice of his existence, the principal joy
of his social life. The largest part of shipyard conversation, beyond the routine of the day's necessities, was
occupied with some aspect of the pleasures or the problems of sex; and shipyard jokes were broad and racy
in the extreme. Emphasized in this interest was the sexual role of women, which influenced every association
between the sexes and surrounded with an atmosphere

of obscure emotionality each area of unfamiliar and unusual coöperation. The emphasis upon sex, moreover, as it evoked the biological distinctions between men and women, also reinforced the lines of social demarcation. Traditions supposedly governing the proper division of labor between men and women were linked with even more profoundly rooted traditions concerning divisions in biological function, and change in the structure of the former might seem to imply a threat to the latter's sacrosanct stability.

In the shipyards, rumor was continually busy with suspicions and reports of salacious activities in the obscurer parts of the ships or in some vaguely identified warehouse. Like evil-smelling breezes, tales of scandal idly floated from group to group: of a stolen kiss or an amusing infatuation; even of the ultimate in sin, with or without price, in the fantastic discomfort of the double bottoms. One persistent report concerned the activities of enterprising professionals for whom a shipyard job was said merely to provide an opportunity for pursuit of a yet more lucrative career. The end result of all such talk, of course, was to deny the possibility of the establishment of businesslike relationships between men and women on the job and to discredit women as effective workers. For women, as the unwelcome intruders, were taxed with all the many and varied disruptions, in the routines of workmanship, that were chargeable against sexual interests and activities. Thus, on my first day of work in the yards I was warned by the superintendent of my craft that any flirting with the men in the yards would result in dire consequences for me. "Remember what I told you," he called after me as I left his office; "give a man an inch and he'll take a mile, and if there's any funny business on the job, it'll be you who goes out like a light."

The restless, sexually interpreted distrust of women as shipyard workers achieved a climax of agitation at Moore Dry Dock in the fall of 1942, a period when the employment of women was becoming an established policy. A highly sensational and much read local newspaper carried a melodramatic indictment of shipyard women by a wife and mother who charged that she had lost her husband to one of the unprincipled breed. The writer, whose eloquence (which smacked of the professional touch) was only excelled by her fervor, proceeded from the specific instance of betrayal to proclaim the general unsuitability of women to the work and environment of the shipyards and announced her conviction that only money-hunger and man-hunger were responsible for their intrusion into this unnatural field of labor. In the mysterious manner of all news of unusual appeal, knowledge of the letter and its content spread throughout the yards within an hour or so after the newspaper appeared, and here and there knots of men or women gathered to discuss the merits of the argument. A sentiment already prevalent in the shipyards had now acquired the added dignity of printed and public statement, and it flourished accordingly.

Following the publication of the letter and the accompanying ferment, word was spread, triumphantly by the disgruntled men and fearfully by many of the women, that as a consequence of feminine misbehavior and unfitness all women, or at least the unmarried ones, were to be summarily dismissed. A few men in authority were not content, however, to await the slow processes of official justice, but took punitive measures into their own hands. One such minor potentate, whose wife, it was said, had complained about the temptations to which he was subjected in the dissolute shipyards, went about among the girls of his jurisdiction with a bottle of acetone and a handkerchief and forced them to remove their nail polish and lipstick, under penalty of his displeasure.

The management issued strict rules to govern the dress of shipyard women—rules based fully as much on the principles of concealment and sexless propriety as on the purported aims of safety. Women guards stalked vigilantly through the warehouses, the workshops, and the rest rooms, looking for the coy curl unconfined by a bandanna, the bejeweled hand, and the revealing sweater. Slip-on sweaters were not to be worn except when modestly covered by a shirt or outer jacket. Hardly out of pure regard for propriety, the women themselves formed an undeputized but effective agency for enforcement of the rules of rude and graceless dress. Shorn of their own adornment, they were quick to pluck others' plumes. A woman of my acquaintance whose job was sedentary and relatively clean came in a suit to her first day of shipyard work, but she needed only one session with the girls of the rest room to convince her that she had best come the second morning in her husband's overalls. In the meantime, of course, the women in the offices at the front of the yard, the typists, the bookkeepers, and the private secretaries, bobbed about in their sweaters and knee-high skirts or swished through the corridors in their svelte and elegant black dresses without arousing any special comment or causing more than a flutter of disturbance in the routine of work. For it was the change, the element of strangeness, that fostered anxiety over the proper dress of women in the industrial jobs. Like soldiers infiltrating enemy lines, women in the shipyards had to be camouflaged lest the difference in sex be unduly noted and emphasized.

Traditional sensitivity to the assumption by women of the untraditional function of breadwinner was multifaceted, and multifaceted too was the structure of rationalization which supported the contrary and corrective dogma that woman's proper sphere of endeavor was the home. It has not, of course, been altogether unusual for women of the working classes, even in America, to respond to the pressure of economic necessity by supplementing the family income through casual and ill-paid labor. But among the workers of the shipyards, who were a step removed from the grinding struggle for mere subsistence, and many of whom were straining yet more ambitiously toward the customs and standards of the middle class, the conviction was widespread that the virility and capacity of a man were brought into question whenever any female dependent in his family, particularly his wife, went out in the world to earn her living. The greater the shipyard worker's economic security, the more determined he was to be the pillar of his family's financial support. The masses of the unskilled, dazzled by the glow of unprecedented wages, might come into the shipyard in family groups and work at the same bench, but I never knew a craftsman whose wife or daughter worked in the shipyards, too. Indeed, it was the frequent boast of such men that they had frustrated with one mighty, forbidding "No!" the foolish desire of their womenfolk to take up the welder's torch. "I told my old lady," one hard-bitten patriarch said, "that if she put foot inside this here shipyard, I'd just stay home myself and take up knitting. There's not going to be two in my family that's working." Another craftsman, of gentler temper, expressed the same dogma in his simple query, "Do they call a woman who works a wife?" To these guardians of tradition, the woman at home, busy at the stove and crib, was not only properly and sufficiently occupied, but also was concrete evidence of her husband's earning capacity—and was more likely to be <u>docile</u> than the woman who had her own pay check to spend as she wished.

Tradition resisted the invasion of the shipyards by women; masculine egotism took part in the resistance; but more obvious, persistent, and perhaps more basic was the fear of women as competitors in a hitherto unchallenged monopoly of men. In an economy where jobs are at a premium and the specter of unemployment never quite vanishes and where at best the price of a skill is subject to decline with every increase in the supply of qualified workers, the entrance of any new group into the field of competition is usually resisted. Even the young male is not greeted with unqualified enthusiasm by established workers, but is forced to thread his way through the maze of apprenticeship before he arrives at full status in his craft. Normally, of course, women were excluded from the official channels of entrance into the trades of heavy industry; with the outbreak of war and its abnormality, the craft unions, hardened in monopoly, stubbornly attempted to protect their exclusiveness against the ever-growing pressure. But since the unions could either accept women into their ranks or watch helplessly while women worked outside their jurisdiction, restrictions were eventually broken through with a speed which depended directly upon the need for man power and the scarcity of it. Great numbers of welders were desperately required, for instance, to serve at the very base of modern ship construction; therefore, the first women hired to work in the crafts at Moore Dry Dock were welders. The need for expansion did not affect my own craft, that of steam-fitting, so violently or so soon, and it was not until September, 1942, that a peremptory order from national headquarters compelled the local union to open its doors to women. Even then, however, the intruders were often given a second-class membership, which in the Steamfitters' Union was compensated by abrogation of half the usual initiation fee, but which in all the craft unions of the shipyard tacitly implied that the emergency, union affiliation, and women's jobs would terminate together.

The reluctance of the unions to permit full participation by women was only the token of the reluctance that was felt, and often spoken, by almost every masculine member. It was not explained by reference to any self-ish desire to protect a vested interest from further sharing. The principal and most common explanation was that the work was unsuitable for women, who, being less vigorous and less reliable than men, were not able to learn and perform the skills of a trade with the same efficiency. Countless anecdotes proved—to the satisfaction of the already prejudiced—that women were hopelessly inept with tools and machinery and were altogether out of place in what had always been the appointed labor of men. One crusty pipefitter exploded when he learned of a certain woman's advancement to journeyman's status. "That big fat slob a pipefitter!" he finally managed to say. "Why, she waddles like a duck, and she handles a wrench like a powder puff. I'd throw a kid helper right off my gang if he couldn't fit a joint better and faster than she'll ever know how to do."

The men seldom credited the women with the capacity or the desire to put in an honest day's work. "Take a look around at the women and what they're doing," one disgruntled workman urged. "From one end of the hull to the other they're jawing or prettying up their faces or bothering some man and keeping him from his work. You ask any man, and he'll tell you that a woman in the shipyards is only in the way. They don't none of them belong here." I remember another captious old codger, a craftsman of seventy-odd years, who was just as much on wartime sufferance in the yards as any woman there. His principal complaint was the uselessness of the women and their continual preoccupation with mirror and lipstick. "Lazy and good-for-nothing, that's what those women are," he pronounced in final judgment. "If I had any say-so in this place, I'd fire every last one of them."

The bitter cup of these malcontents was made yet more unpalatable: for doing less than a man's work—much less, in their opinion—the women nonetheless received a man's full pay. It was a conviction almost universal among the men that if women had to be introduced into the industry for lack of desirable males, it should only be as inferiors whose wages were in accord with their capacities. I found no man who would accept as valid the argument that the security of the standard wage would be threatened if women were customarily paid less for doing the same type, if not always the same quality or quantity, of work as the men, since to employers the greater skill of the man might frequently be outweighed by the woman's smaller wage. Against the concrete wall of masculine assurance that no employer could ever prefer a woman, even at half the wage, the argument was about as penetrating as birdshot.

Woman's claim to the good working conditions of the shipyard was likewise attacked as inherently unjust. The good wages and hours were the product of long, arduous, and sometimes bloody struggle by men. Women had played no part in the organized effort by which the struggle had been won, and were assumed not to understand the principles involved; they were thought to be passively disinterested at best, and often actively unsympathetic. The union-conscious worker looked with jaundiced eye upon both their presence in a highly organized industry and their nominal membership in the respectable unions of the crafts. Like an unassimilated minority within a threatened nation, women, he feared, might prove a grave source of weakness in the event of attack by an exteral enemy.

This skepticism was especially strong in a skilled craftsman, long active in union affairs of the.Bay Area, with whom I had many heated discussions on the subject. "Women don't know how to be loyal to a union," he asserted. "They're born, and they grow up, dirty dealers. There isn't a straight one among 'em." To illustrate his contention he recounted his unhappy experience, in the depression, at attempting to organize the clerks of a local dime store. "I slaved for those girls," he declared, "and after I'd helped get them the wage boost they wanted, they wouldn't look at me for dirt. When I'd done for them all I'd done, and they told me, with my cards right there ready to be signed, that their boss was a nice fellow and they couldn't hurt his feelings by joining a lousy union, well, I felt like pasting one of 'em square on the jaw."

Entering into every established craft as helpers only, women faced peculiar and discriminatory difficulties in advancing to a higher status. So far as came to my knowledge, women at Moore Dry Dock did not pass beyond the status of journeyman to the supervisory positions of leaderman or quarterman except in the despised craft of the general laborer. Further advancement was blocked by the refusal of men to work under a woman's direction. As a general policy, indeed, women were not advanced to journeyman unless it were possible to provide enough women helpers to accomplish the necessary labor without the aid of a man's greater strength. I soon learned what difficulties awaited a woman given authority over shipyard men. Assigned to a warehouse staffed mainly by older workers on the downgrade, I was presently advanced to a position of slightly increased responsibility and better pay. The protest of those who were passed by was immediate and sharp. The boss was hounded with complaints, and I was a target for sour glances and surly remarks. One disgusted fellow replied to my request for help in moving a three-hundred-pound box of pipe fittings with the brusque comment, "If you get a man's pay, I guess you can do a man's work for it." Weeks of time, every device of tact, and feminine sweetness were required to return the atmosphere to its normal calm.

Women were frequently shifted from boss to boss, finding a permanent place at last only on a job so routine or unpleasant as not to attract the more favored

men. In any period of slowdown or changeover, discriminatory layoffs were likely to be made, and in the
winter of 1943, after an important and labor-demand-
ing contract had been completed at Moore Dry Dock, a
large group of women electricians were forced to accept either a release or a pay reduction—from the
amount to which their seniority had entitled them to the
basic helper's wage. A year later, disproportional quitting and layoffs of the women were clearly to be seen
in the statistics of employment for the entire shipyard.
By February, 1945, women working in the crafts at
Moore Dry Dock constituted less than ten per cent of
the total personnel. Only thirteen hundred yet remained
of the seven thousand who had filled the yards with
femininity during the period of peak employment a
year and a half before. Masculine hopes for total exclusion of the intruding group were well on the way to fulfillment.

Only once did a man in authority seek to anticipate
the slow workings of circumstance and to execute with
one bold stroke what many another doubtless often
wished to do. In the spring of 1944 this resolute character, a supervising foreman of machinists, risked the
displeasure of governmental agencies and even of the
union in control of his craft when, with the barest
shadow of explanation, he fired all the women under
his jurisdiction. The work was unsuitable for women;

it was too arduous and too dirty: thus he parried official inquiry. But private conversation revealed his violent contempt of women, the real basis for his act. When one mild-mannered woman, urged by her immediate superior, attempted to intercede for herself since she liked and needed her job, the foreman started up from his desk in vehement refusal. "Women are no good at all in the shipyards," he shouted. "They're lazy and shiftless, and they have to make all the men around them useless, too. I've finally got rid of the women in my department, and I don't want any of them back. It's too bad every skirt in Moore Dry Dock can't be given her quit slip right now." Thus were expressed the unspoken or temporarily ineffective thoughts of most of his fellows.

The woman, pioneer intruder though she might be, was usually unaware of the significance of her role and unconcerned with its responsibilities. She brought with her the attitudes and practices which had suited her previous environment. By her own unthinking, therefore, she often contributed to the antagonism. Many women were no more than young and adventuresome girls, their normal boy-centered lives rent asunder by war, who turned to the shipyards primarily for excited roving among droves of draft-exempt men. The older women were often merely fleeing the housewife's routine, which had grown dull over the years; and for

them, too, the function of the shipyard, aside from sup-
plying the weekly pay check, was to provide release
from emotional frustration and satisfy vague personal
hungers. Sex apparently was a more persistent preoccupation of the shipyard woman than of the shipyard man,
and the talk of the women, their clothing, and their behavior, were calculated to maintain the emphasis upon
their role as sexually attractive creatures. Giddy charm-
ers skirted the bare fringe of the management's dress
regulations, and by a variety of cunning devices succeeded in revealing as much as possible of the delights
beneath. (One such was wont to say with titillating gusto
that underneath her well-fitting and well-filled overalls
she wore "nothing, nothing at all—it's every bit just
me.") The scrawls and graphic illustrations penciled
on the walls of the rest rooms for "ladies" were additional proof that at least some of the women in the shipyards completely justified masculine rumor and insult.
Philandering did occur, furthermore, and homes were
broken and occasional irate wives or husbands raged
against the temptations and sins of the shipyards and
particularly against the presence there of the adventure-
seeking woman and the vastly experimental unmarried
girl, with sound personal reasons for their anger.

Still another masculine indictment was well supported by observable fact, for the work attitudes of
many women who retained in this new situation their

accustomed dependence upon feminine prerogative did not meet the standards of the craftsman. Women in the shipyards, even while they assumed the rights of equality, also cherished the privileges of the protected status; they sought to eat their cake and keep their figures too. The heavy piece of pipe was lifted, the dirty task was accomplished, not by honest sweat, but with a coy smile and the toss of a pretty head. Advancement could be won in the same manner. Seldom did a sense of responsibility to the job obstruct this desire to ease through the working day. Looking upon their work as temporary—a respite preceding either marriage or the return of the drafted husband,—women for the most part had little impulse to delve into the secrets of their craft or to work any harder than was absolutely necessary. They were hampered, finally, by consciousness of their previous inexperience and an attendant sense of inadequacy. Few women would have disputed seriously the masculine claim of their inferiority in the industrial arts, and even fewer, however much they might hope to have the chance, actually expected that they would continue in their shipyard crafts once the pressure of war should be relaxed.

Here and there a woman worker, happy in the craft which she was learning and somewhat heady with her economic independence, would be torn between the claims of home and job in deciding a course to follow

if freedom to choose were hers. But normally the women
kept, in their spoken statements at any rate, to the well-
worn pathways. Many, indeed, were as fervid as the
men in their antagonism to ideas which implied equality of economic opportunity. I overheard one proclaim
that the members of her sex had no right to compete
with men for jobs. "They can't do the work as well as
a man, anyway," she continued. "They don't have the
brains of men, and they don't have the strength." Most
of the women around her were useless and their employment was a waste of money, she asserted; as soon
as veterans should return, women workers ought to
go. She herself was eager to see the end of the war.
"I'd rather be at home, besides," she concluded. "My
husband would be happier, and so would I." Another
woman wanted laws to compel married women, in periods of job scarcity such as the recent depression at least,
to relinquish all paid employment and return home.
"A married woman's first duty is to her home and family," she elaborated. "And you can't have a job and
keep a home as well."

This attitude was the more readily accepted by the
women because shipyard labor possessed few of the
attractions in terms of personal development or expression which a profession or business holds for members
of the middle class. The job of the shipyard man was
customarily counted among the necessities and not the

joys of his life. Day after day its irksome routine was endured primarily for the sake of the livelihood it afforded; it was a means to an end and not an end in itself. Hence with no great regret women could retreat in thought and eventually in person to the enjoyment and enrichment of a home for the material needs of which the husband's labors might provide. "I'm going to quit this shipyard the minute the war is over," a woman busy sweeping a ship's steel deck announced. "I'm going home where I can be warm and comfortable and away from all this dirt. Let my husband be the sucker and slave away the rest of his days. I'm going to be a lady."

And yet, these women worked! Despite their own reluctance and inadequacy, despite the derision which surrounded them and which their own attitudes helped to maintain, thousands of women came, remained for a year, for two years, and began to disappear only when the pressing need for them had passed. Among them, moreover, were some who gave the lie to tradition. Two women electricians, after months of attentive apprenticeship, were made responsible for installing the wiring in an electrically operated steering gear upon which the very function of the ship must depend. A girl pipefitter wept with chagrin when a leak was discovered in the piping she had installed. With some hesitancy men admitted the efficiency of these and other women like them, and gave them grudging praise for work well done. One foreman confessed that a few of his women workers were superior to the average run of men. "Those women feel that they have to be better than the men," he explained, "because they know they're on trial in the shipyards, and so far as I'm concerned they sure have passed the test." I chanced upon several fair-minded men who as the result of personal experience had come to believe that women had a permanent place in certain phases of heavy industry; that their work as electricians, for instance, was good enough to assure them equal consideration with men in a free field of competition. "There's some work around the yards women haven't got the strength to do," said one judicious observer, "but there's a lot of other things they can do just as well as men. Women make good electricians, good sheet-metal workers, and in the machine shop they handle some of the smaller lathes all right. Any boss will tell you that as storekeepers they're even better than men because they've got more sense of neatness and system and they don't get fretful sitting in one place."

Even over the broad field where outstanding excellence and indisputable capacity could play no part, a variety of wartime pressures were at work upon established attitudes, and both men and women responded to a degree, the women with greater diligence and fuller appreciation of workmanship, the men with increased tolerance. The mere confinement and enforced association of the shipyard brought the transition part way. Then, too, the labor of shipyard women was sorely needed. Propaganda was directed at the points of conflict to hasten the transition. To the staff of the Moore Dry Dock Company were added counselors whose function was to encourage women to enter the shipyards, to adjust to the environment, and thereby to become and remain effective workers. At the height of early agitation against the increasing employment of women a short-lived women's council was formed, so that the women workers themselves might air their grievances to company representatives and, in turn, become disseminators of company policy. Finally, in late spring, 1943, an orientation program was set up, through which almost all newly entering women were compelled to pass before being initiated into the actual work of the yards. It consisted of two weeks of intensive training and indoctrination in the technique of the shipyard crafts and the mores of shipyard society. Hopelessly inadequate women were, of course, eliminated. Thus the management tried to smooth the rough edges and to remind women that intruders in a man's world must live as much as possible by man's code.

Less directly, the sanctions of the state were brought to bear, and there were men at Moore Dry Dock who

acknowledged a change of heart after observing some
official's public praise of women's work in ordnance
plant, aircraft factory, and shipyard. Indeed, the conventional prejudices were under continual bombard-
ment from newspapers, radios, magazines, and motion
pictures, which all combined to establish Rosie the
Riveter as a heroine. A few of the more liberal unions
also aided in the program to the extent of encouraging
active participation by women in union affairs, insuring
their rights to seniority and advancement on the job, and
promising consideration of their interests in the search
for future employment. The Bay Area local of the
Steamfitters' Union, guided by a broad-visioned leadership, actually elected a woman shipyard worker to its
executive board.

Nonetheless, it was apparent as the shipyard community declined in size and approached normality
that the unprecedented relationships between men and
women which wartime work entailed, and the unusual
unity which encompassed for a period the interests and
labors of both sexes, were to be in large part reabsorbed
into the dominant pattern of tradition. Partly as a result
of their own uninstructed choice of familiar limitations,
and partly as a result of masculine determination to
preserve the policy of exclusion, women remained, at
the end of the shipyard experience of widened opportunity, as at the beginning, a minority group on the

fringes of the industrial field. Still beyond the horizon was the day when a woman might be trained as an electrician or a welder and might confidently expect equal consideration with a man on the basis of capacity alone. To this degree the citizenship of women continued to be conditional and their status to fall short of complete equality with men in a man's world. For although the conventional alignment of the two sexes was rudely shaken in the shipyard situation and some of the barriers between their separate spheres were displaced and weakened, there was no evidence that principles of unity were established by this period of disturbance which were strong enough to withstand the backwash to old and earnestly cherished distinctions.

OKIES

❦👉 IMMIGRATION from foreign shores, the principal source of the nation's growth during the nineteenth and early twentieth centuries, has had a more recent, concentrated resurgence in the populating of the three states of the Pacific Coast. California in particular has been fed and fattened by migration. Asia and Mexico have supplied some of the needed man power for the increasing demands of the State, but most of California's immigrants—recently almost all—have been foreign only in being non-Californian. For almost a generation, now, restrictions upon immigration have enabled the nation to achieve stability; but California has remained restless. Between 1900 and 1940, while the population of the entire country increased by 73 per cent, that of California increased 365 per cent. A survey conducted in 1944 showed that not less than 80 per cent of the inhabitants of Los Angeles were born elsewhere.

Though industrial and agricultural interests welcomed and on occasion busily encouraged the recurrent waves of migration which replenished their reservoirs of man power, and though the land itself with its undeveloped resources called for more and yet more hands to delve and build and irrigate, the stranger in this society of strangers was nonetheless notoriously disdained. Especially when his skin was not unsullied white, the newcomer in California usually met with a rude reception (save for a time, perhaps, from the promoters who imported him), as the State's long history of anti-Chinese, anti-Japanese, and anti-Mexican agitation amply demonstrates. But barriers of distrust and discrimination were likewise raised against the white man and the American whose origins were in some other and less favored area. Those who came early frowned upon those who chanced to come late, and, further documenting a common human tendency, denied to them, whatever their merits or their claims, full access to the privileges of the established community. The arrogance of the native son was solidified, as in few if any other states of the Union, into a policy of contempt and rejection of the immigrant, and enthusiasts endeavored to compensate for the youthfulness of their homeland by the violence with which they defended it from the stranger's desecration.

In the late years of the depression a migratory movement into California occurred which had its source in the states of the Southwest where the final crushing blow of the drought had fallen upon a people already bowed and weakened by the burdens of financial chaos. Large parts of the agricultural areas of Oklahoma, Texas, Missouri, and Arkansas were prostrated by this double catastrophe; and westward to the groves and vineyards of California trekked a multitude of the disestablished.

"Okies" these migrants were loosely called, for the former homes of many were the burned-out farms of Oklahoma. The manner of their reception in California has been well publicized.

The Okies came to California at a time when the protective impulses of its economy were at fever pitch in a situation of insufficiency. As a propertyless group they offered none of the compensations for hospitality which certain interested citizens might find in the individual of means who chose to travel or to settle in the State and freely spend his former earnings there, or even in the practiced workmen whose skill might ordinarily be useful. California's traditional exclusiveness became an active antagonism against this new invasion; and the Okies who ventured hopefully across the mountain barriers found no remedy for wretchedness after all. Amid the riches of a prosperous domain they still clung with starveling fingers to the mere shreds of life.

Unwelcome though they were, this group of migrants, like the many who had preceded them, existed somehow through the first few difficult years and remained in California. In course of time the Okies became relatively integrated members of the small agricultural centers in which they settled. The surrounding citizenry made its grudging peace with them, and, with the steadily increasing prosperity of the region, the Okies themselves came to be less obviously branded by their poverty and degradation. Numbers of them moved from their shantytowns into the respectable homes of respectable neighborhoods and were enabled to adopt many other elements of the camouflage of convention. But the tradition of the Okie, and his wretchedness, having a vigor of its own, still persisted, and was ready, when war brought new migrants, to envelop them, too, in shame and derision.

As war approached, there suddenly were too few willing hands to keep the fires of California's revitalized industry alight. The indigent and labor-seeking immigrant, previously discouraged and abused, was now welcomed, sought after, and often stood, a puzzled and passive prize, between rival claimants for his services. Agencies throughout the country recruited workmen for the aircraft factories and shipyards of California, as imaginative industrialists cast forth nets and gathered in catches by the trainload. Between April, 1940, and November, 1943, nearly a million and a half people crossed the borders of California and were drawn into its war industries. Every state contributed to this pilgrimage, but the Southwest was once again the principal source. Almost half of those who came to California to work at the Kaiser shipyards at Richmond were natives of Oklahoma, Arkansas, and Texas; with Missouri added to this list, the same proportion holds for a sampling conducted at Moore Dry Dock. On the basis of these analyses it may safely be estimated that at least twenty per cent of the workers in the Bay Area shipyards were Okies; in the aircraft factories of southern California, where the work was less well paid and presumably less skilled, the proportion was probably even higher.

These Okies were of somewhat different type and background from those of the earlier exodus. Farm life was not absent from their experience, but most of them had at least a smattering of industrial skill acquired in their own small towns and in oil fields. They journeyed, moreover, under the aegis of far more favorable circumstances than those which had accompanied the trek of their predecessors. Theirs was not the futile flight from misery, but a confident journey toward a definite goal for which they were to some degree already prepared. And yet, the brand of "stranger" was plain upon them; those who had settled earlier in California—or perhaps had been conceived and born there—were as quick as they had been before to make the traditional gestures of rejection. For the Okie, though white and American, had peculiarities that set him clearly apart. His dialect—not quite the twang of the Midwest nor the drawl of the Deep South, but a composite of both—was one of the most prominent. His dress tended to be flamboyant, and his manner likewise. He fancied himself on a horse and on the wide, uncitied plains of his native region. But whatever the traits which marked him off, he was undeniably different, and upon the basic cloth of this difference the varying patterns of aversion were readily embroidered.

I had not worked long at Moore Dry Dock before I became aware of the Okies as a minority group with their own burden of disapproval and discrimination. Much of the derision aimed at them was intermingled with heavy humor, which made the more likely its frequent and open expression. Scarcely a day passed without my hearing of the Okie and his idiosyncrasies, and though laughter softened the impact of the remarks, the undercurrent of conscious ridicule was steady. There were jocose tales, for instance, of the money-hunger of the Okies, too avid to be respectable, which led them to travel west and seek employment as family units—husband, wife, grandma, half-grown youngsters, and all. Of an Okie family well represented at Moore Dry Dock one man remarked, "Why, they'd put their five-year-old to work if they could get him through the hiring office as a midget." It was said that Okies were in the shipyards and in the State only to gather in the golden harvest while the war bloom lasted; that done, they would shake the hated dust from their feet and hurry home to Oklahoma—or Texas or Missouri,—where their wealth could buy half a county or an oil well and they could be permanently affluent. The contrary charge was also made: they were improvident wastrels whose extravagance would result, once the shipyards ceased to function and a man had really to earn his livelihood, in their complete reliance upon public charity. Whichever process occurred, of course, the man who considered himself a Californian might base his indignation upon an equal sense of imposition and descent.

Antagonism to the shipyard Okie, like antagonism to the shipyard woman, dwelt within the structure of the jealous guarding of a vested interest, and many of the barbed arrows of contempt were shot from that sturdy fortress in the rear. Okies, like women, furthermore, were assumed to know little or nothing of the techniques of industry and to be scarcely capable of learning more. The depression-born tradition of the wretchedness and incompetence of the Okie was too firmly implanted to be easily disturbed by new and conflicting facts. "The Okies are a low class of people," was the summing up of one commentator, who also insisted that he could distinguish native Okies by their physical appearance alone. "They have a different kind of face," he said; "more dumb-looking, somehow." Many workers testified, when I questioned them, that the Okie was neither as well educated nor as intelligent as the average American. "Hardly any of them have gone to the eighth grade in school," one critic remarked. "They're too dumb to get that far."

Okie stupidity was second only to sex as a subject for scrawls on bulkheads and toilet-shack walls. One of the milder examples was the caption, "Okie, this is a door," crudely chalked over an obvious bulkhead passageway. In a rougher vein of satire, shipyard urinals, I was told, were frequently labeled, "Okie drinking fountain," and a tin cup was conveniently placed near by. Half humorously, half maliciously, the symbol of the Okie was elaborated with countless details of stupidity, so that he emerged at last a caricature of a man whose only proper sphere of living was the outhouse and the tumbledown shanty of the funny-paper Ozarks.

The union-conscious worker had his own peculiar reason for complaint against the intruding Okies: in the excellent wages and good working conditions of the shipyards they were reaping the rewards of the toil and sacrifice of others. Again as with respect to shipyard women, concern was also widely felt lest the Okies, whose status in the unions was unqualified by any formal limitations, would through ignorance and misconduct abuse their union privileges to the permanent detriment of the organizations. Many old-timers in the craft unions shook their heads in doubt over the vast wartime expansion of union membership; they saw the spore of decay in it, and spoke of the newcomers, the Okies in particular, as the source of eventual union collapse. It was said that the Okies joined the unions and paid their dues only because they were compelled to do so, that they had no knowledge of the benefits and principles of union coöperation, and furthermore, that they were not interested in being enlightened. "I don't know why the Okies are that way," one shipyard worker with some background of union experience complained. "Maybe it's because they've been farmers all their lives. They just don't understand what a union means, and when they come into one they only know how to destroy it."

In the Steamfitters' Union, whose membership included no Negroes and in which women, because the work was heavy, were never considered a permanent threat to job tenure, Okies were the main targets for the resentments of the long-established ruling clique whose job monopoly had hitherto been secure. In the many meetings that I attended, every difficulty that was discussed, from treasury deficits to jurisdictional disputes, was squarely placed, by some indignant member, on the cluttered doorstep of the Okie. When the sick benefits were stopped for lack of funds, it was the Okies, always on charity, who had misused their rights. When the machinists had a job which the steamfitters claimed for themselves, it was once again because some ignorant Okie had given the work away. In this union, the Okie issue reached its turbulent climax in a bitterly contested election of officers. The champions of exclusiveness flung the epithet of "Okie" broadside at their opposition, which indeed had sprung from the vastly swollen ranks of new members in the union. The epithet had no desired effect, however; the old-timers went down to ignominious defeat—proclaiming that it was Okie greed and trickery which had bested them and which in time would wreck the union.

It was apparent, especially in this campaign, that the term "Okie" was not used with precision. No clear boundary of color separated the Okies, and since their traits were so apt to disappear with time, the loose use of the term was understandable. Often it was planted on any newcomer who was uncitified, unskilled, accustomed to a low standard of living, and who threatened the economic security of the older resident. Or, even more broadly, it became an epithet to hurl at any unwelcome stranger, provided he was white and American and could not easily be made the butt of a more violent appellation. I once called a shipyard worker to task for the unjustifiability of his attack upon the Okies, and referred to several of them, known to both of us, who by no means corresponded with the portrait he was painting. "But," he explained to me, "I'm not talking about Jim or George or Bill; they're all right even if they were born in Oklahoma or Arkansas. It's the real Okies I'm talking about, those good-for-nothings who came to California in hard times and lived like animals along the highway, and the lazy, ignorant fellows who fill the shipyards now and who won't even lift a broom to earn their livings honestly. It's a kind of people I'm talking about, no matter where they came from."

The Okies as I knew them, however, did not conform in any consistent fashion to the symbol cherished by common opinion. They were, to be sure, less well schooled as a group than the average resident of more favored areas. Among them were remarkable examples of ignorance and lack of opportunity, men and women who could scarcely write their own names and numbers, whose formal education had been halted at the third or fourth grade. "Back where I come from we poor folks couldn't go to school," remarked one graying Oklahoma woman, in shamefaced explanation. "In spring there was the planting and the weeding of the cotton, in fall the picking, and in winter we had no shoes." Among them, also, were hayseeds who retained their barnyard crudities of custom and their barnyard superstitions. I recall a raw-boned farmer, Texas-born and Texas-bred, who with all the weight of gospel truth proclaimed that if a successful crop were to be obtained, potato cuttings could be planted only in the dark phase of the moon. Unaware of the depth of such irrationality, since at the time I was too new to the yards, I suggested the desirability of experimentation to test the validity of his claim. The wall of his faith was absolute and unassail-

[handwritten margin note: That's interesting]

[handwritten margin note: She doesn't seem that impressed either]

able; I might as well have requested that he walk off the stage rigger's scaffolding to discover whether the force of gravity would really pull him to the ground.

Actuality even exceeded legend in one Okie women, Beulah; her voice, through years of hog and children calling, had attained to almost incredible power and stridency, and her manner was all outward-going noise, bluster, and uncultivated good will. She employed the unassisted equipment of nature when she blew her nose; she was master of perhaps a little more than a third-grader's skill in calligraphy and English spelling; she believed firmly in miraculous cures for warts and dog bites, and the world was a never-ending source of wonder to her naïve and curious gaze. She had spent her life in the cotton fields of her native state, and now the city where a lucky chance had brought her—grown woman though she was, and the mother of grown sons—was a great and gaudy toy with which she never tired of playing. She wandered airily through the mazes of the local variety stores, bought a jigsaw puzzle here (which she would surely have to frame, it was that pretty!) and some scarlet drinking glasses there, because they sparkled brightly in the light. And always she wearied the patience of her fellow shipyard workers on the following day by listing and relisting in minute and loving detail her numerous purchases and small adventures. Yet even Beulah was not everything an Okie was reported and supposed to be. She was most emphatically not lazy. She had watered a thousand cotton fields with the flood of her energy, and she saw no reason to dam the torrent now. Despite the fact that Beulah was the frequent butt of ridicule and caustic humor from those who heard the clamor of her voice or chanced but briefly to observe her more peculiar customs, she had her shipyard friends as well, who, having pierced the rough externals of an Okie culture, had glimpsed the common humanity at the core.

The Okie group, however, in its geographical sense was by no means entirely composed of hayseeds, hillbillies, and unsophisticated illiterates. Many, who had worked in Southwestern towns, oil fields, and industrialized cities, were conversant enough with skilled trades to hold positions of responsibility. Discrimination against the Okie in terms of upgrading was seldom if ever practiced; and if his knowledge warranted, an Okie was almost as free as anyone else who lacked the advantage of prewar employment in the yards to mount the ascending steps of the industrial hierarchy. The Okie bosses whom I knew were well-liked men whose origins were not considered. One steamfitter boss, whose birthplace, as all who knew him were aware, was a small Oklahoma town, was accepted without qualification in shipyard society. He, too, had made the wartime trek, but he was distinguished by an economic and cultural background much better than average, which included even a year or two of technical training at the university of his home state. By penetrating the confines of the middle class he had also stepped completely out of the Okie category and all that it implied. I never heard anyone, except the man himself when in a jesting mood, use "Okie" in reference to him or his activities. Okies in humbler places were often equally well regarded both by their supervisors and by the men with whom they worked. My own boss often remarked of one of his more skilled and diligent workers, "I don't care if that fellow is an Okie, he's the best man I've got on my gang." The very vagueness of the boundaries of the Okie habitat gave the epithet of "Okie" a general use and at the same time allowed many persons to escape entirely from the circle of disapproval and become accepted members of the adopted community.

The Okie, moreover, even though he at first conformed with his tradition, adjusted easily and soon to many standards of his new environment, and became less readily identifiable. The richness and variety of life in the large cities soon raised the level of his material tastes. As shipyard wages weighed more and more heavily in Okie pockets, there was a customary progression from dime-and-dollar palaces of gauds and baubles to working-class-conscious outfitters by mail order and credit, to vast emporiums which with the quantity and

variety of their wares sought to attract the widest possible buying public, and sometimes even to the final
pinnacle of expensive tastes, the fur salons and perfume
shops of the most exclusive stores. This willingness to
accept, this eagerness, indeed, to obtain the gifts of fortune which hitherto had been beyond their reach, was
implicit in the Okies' determination to remain permanently on the Pacific Coast. Casual conversations and
careful statistical surveys alike showed that, although a
few were nostalgic enough to return to their childhood
homes when the yards should shut down, most of them
believed they had reached a better world—certainly a
world of higher wages—and had no intention of retrac-
ing their steps.

The Okies were aware of the attacks against them;
contemplating, as so many of them did, permanent settlement in the land of the enemy, they developed a coun-
teroffensive. A few of the more sensitive became sullen;
they withdrew into self-chosen segregation and were capable, when disturbed, of utterances against the pride-
ful Californians which were quite as scathing as any
ever hurled against the Okies. The exclusive Californian was declared to be unjust, morally inferior, and as
hospitable as a dog in the manger. "Why, back in my
home town," drawled one offended Okie, "we treat stray
dogs better than they treat men out here." The Californians, it was further pointed out, had little basis for

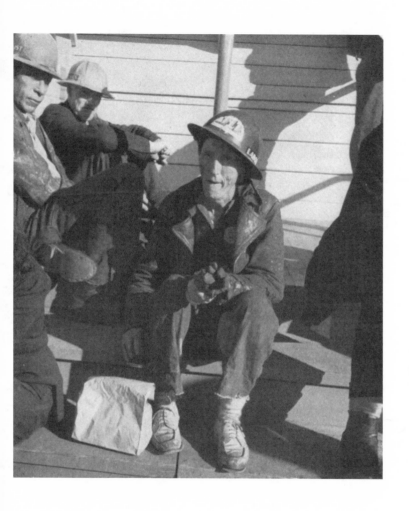

their pride since most of them were imigrants themselves, with only the grace of a few more years to make
the difference, and the rest had origins which, even if
native, would hardly bear close scrutiny. It was an Okie
who acquainted me with this rollicking ditty:

> The miners came in forty-nine,
> The whores in fifty-one;
> And when they bunked together
> They begot the native son.

nice

In further satisfaction, the Okies exchanged epithet for
epithet and designated inhospitable Californians as
"Calies" or "Prunepickers," though these terms, too,
were saved from the heaviness of unqualified insult by
a large admixture of bantering good humor and conscious satire.

The more discerning Okies did not depend entirely
upon counteraggression for their defense. Having penetrated the popular concept of the Okie, they were quick
to show where it did not apply. One man felt that *Grapes
of Wrath* had brought about an unjustified impression
of the Okie in the public mind and had done more harm
than good. "Why, all the people in my state aren't like
the people in that book," he protested. "Only a few of
them are so poor and shiftless, and they, mostly, can't
help themselves." The loud-mouthed, vulgar spendthrift, the ignorant and slovenly country hick, and all
the other miserable characters who together were pre-

sumed to represent the Okie group, were no more than types whose habitats could just as well be Colorado, Maine, or Iowa. "There are native California Okies, too," one Southwesterner declared; "I know a lot of them myself." *that's interesting*

Despite occasional verbal skirmishes between the Okie newcomers and the threatened defenders of a longer tenure, the Okies of the wartime immigration, even as I watched them in their first few shipyard years, promised to be quietly absorbed, eventually, into the matrix of California culture. Most of them possessed advantages for adjustment to the new environment which quite overbalanced the fact that, unlike the Okie migrants of an earlier period, they also possessed the necessary means for returning home. They consciously chose to stay and to accept such limitations of income and opportunity as might confront them in the postwar period. Their decision was no doubt the more confidently achieved since it was already evident in the shipyards that, whatever limitations might be built around the Okies as a group, well-adjusted individuals could escape and be admitted into the privileged milieu. And although for the Okies, as for the women industrial workers, the shipyard might represent a high-water mark in economic status and breadth of opportunity, from which a certain recession could be expected after the war, the backwash, at least for the Okies, would hardly be far or long-lasting. The Okies were merely the latest large addition to the population of a state which had grown through the reception of repeated waves of immigration. Since the Okies were distinguished from the older residents by no indelible or hereditary traits, there was every reason to expect that the entire issue of antagonism to the Okie as a type of stranger would in time cease to be of public concern and would come to be preserved at last only in the harmless fossil of a joke. ⟹ true?

So was Okie really a regionless distinction → was this a precursor to "white trash"?

NEGROES

STABILITIES of Negro-white relationships which had been building since the emancipation of the Negro were badly shaken in the course of World War I. One consequence of this earlier world conflict was the creation in the industrialized cities of the North of an intense and sudden need for large quantities of unskilled labor which unlimited supplies of European immigrants were no longer available to fill. Into this vacuum the Southern Negro flowed as naturally as a river to the sea. Within the four years between 1916 and 1920 more than half a million Negroes crowded into Northern cities, where, settling at the bottom levels of the industrial process, they yet could claim a foothold in a new and freer world. And despite the sharp depression of the early 'twenties, the hardships of which fell upon the Negro group with particular severity, no sizable proportion of the migrants sought return to old securities, but instead fresh floods of Negroes came pouring from the South to swell the Northern colonies by a hundred thousand new inhabitants a year.

This first migration of the Southern Negro was halted at the threshold of the depression of the 'thirties, and the next decade constituted a period of relatively peaceful consolidation for the Negro colonies in the North.

But in 1941 and 1942 another war boom struck the nation with many times the impact of the last, and once again expanding industry turned to the Negroes, wherever they could be found, as a group whose labor potential, rich beyond prediction, had hardly been touched. Those already in the industrial areas were the first resource of man power, but the gates of the South soon had to be opened again to allow another exodus from the cotton and tobacco fields. This time, too, the Negroes moved to the arsenals and foundries of the Northeast; but the man-power hunger of the shipyards and aircraft factories of the Far West was greater still. In the first three years of war the Negro population of the Pacific States was swollen by more than one hundred fifty thousand new arrivals, most of whom crowded into the restless cities of California.

Thousands of new Negro inhabitants, for the most part fresh from the South, were employed in the shipyards of the Bay Area—too many to be confined within the black belts already sanctioned by custom. They pressed into surrounding districts, and white residents fled before them as before the coming of a plague. Home owners watched property values fall; in the embattled border regions an owner would frequently indicate a desire to sell only to whites—while he himself moved to a securer neighborhood. Confusion followed chaos when Negroes already living in the community were reported to have spread no mat of welcome for the un-couth newcomers, who were thus denied free use of the one path of adjustment they had counted upon. From the moment of their arrival they were reminded by in-numerable slights that they were not considered as de-sirable guests.

The Negroes at Moore Dry Dock comprised about twenty per cent of the total personnel during the period of peak employment. Most of them were probably strangers in the area, for they lived in the housing projects constructed by the company, a privilege not available to those who had accommodations within com-muting distance of the yards. Though a few of the new-comers were from smaller California towns and some were from Detroit and Chicago, most of them (about eighty per cent, one director of company housing esti-mated) were from the South and Southwest, from Texas, Mississippi, and from Louisiana in particular. Indeed, for reasons no one explained, Moore Dry Dock Com-pany was phenomenally favored by Negroes from Bas-trop, a Louisiana town of five thousand inhabitants. "You ask them where they're from," said a personnel assistant, "and almost every one of them replies, 'Ah's f'om Bastrup, ma'am.' "

Negroes at Moore's were mainly employed for rela-tively unskilled labor—clean-up and maintenance work, rigging, welding, plate-hanging, and other crafts of ship construction as contrasted with those of outfitting and repair. But representatives of the race were to be found in every major trade except steamfitting and pipefitting, from which union regulations excluded them. On the hulls and in the shops, Negroes and whites coöperated in countless tasks, white shoulders straining beside black, and to a casual observer the relationships of the two races seemed miraculously free from tension. The slightest touch, however, revealed the impermanence of the surface calm and the depth of the hatred beneath. In most of the whites the hatred was basic, a deep-seated and strong-flavored aversion that was evident in almost every gesture or remark which was not retarded by the Negro's presence and supposed readiness to take violent revenge for insults. The Negro was seldom even named in all-white talk except in appellations of implied derogation and antagonism, the most common being the timeworn "nigger" and the more recent "jigaboo" or "zigaboo," frequently shortened to "jig" and "zig."

The yard was at the edge of the Negro district of Oakland, and the hostilities of one area reinforced those of the other. It was, of course, assumed that walking through this neighborhood at night was unsafe for a white woman, even the most horny-handed shipyard Amazon. The dark streets and their dark-skinned inhabitants were believed to be the breeding ground of whatever crimes afflicted the city. Until proof positive to the contrary was available, the universal shipyard solution for all rape, robbery, and murder mysteries was, in effect, *cherchez le nègre*. The more shocking and savage the crime, the more certain was Negro participation asserted to be. On the occasion of a kidnaping which occupied newspaper headlines in the fall of 1942, the general surmise among shipyard workers, who were greatly exercised about the crime, was that a Negro had stolen the child away and no doubt murdered her. The talk stopped abruptly, but with no expressions of regret for mistaken judgment, when the child was found alive and well with the white couple who had taken her. Whenever Negroes were authentically implicated in robbery, arson, or beer-hall riots, occurrences which the local press, aware of the tastes of its readers, would seldom neglect to feature, shipyard workers relished the new support for already unassailable illogic. After hearing the bloody details of a fatal encounter between a Negro and his jealous sweetheart, one man sagely shook his head and said, "It just goes to show that niggers take to murder and cutting people up with knives like a duck takes to water. They're natural-born gangsters and criminals."

Knowing little of the ramifications of prejudice, I attempted at first to deal rationally with its more ridiculous outbursts among my fellows. I sought to bring unreasoning antagonism into the field of fair-minded discussion. "Haven't you ever known a Negro who was pleasant, likable, a good worker, and a good fellow?" I would ask a group excited by the most recent Negro-baiting tale. "Oh, sure," someone might reply, "I've known a couple of niggers who were all right enough. I don't mind any of them if they keep their place." Buoyed by partial success, I continued my meager efforts hopefully through the first few months. Then came a sudden storm—an experience sufficient for a lifetime.

Among the workers of the immediate circle in which I worked was Beulah, the classical Okie. Southern rearing had given her an extreme and blatant hostility to the Negro. On the other hand, she was abnormally sensitive to the ridicule which her origin brought upon her. On the morning of the incident, Beulah came to work more than usually agitated. A bystander, jostled in a crowded streetcar, had turned to her and remarked that if only a few of the shipyard Okies, such as she so plainly was, would "go back where they came from," there might be room for the people who belonged in California to ride to work in comfort. It was a rude affront, and I was quick to agree that she should resent it. The people of Oklahoma, I willingly conceded, were surely as American and surely as privileged to ride on streetcars as anyone else. But, falling victim to my own enthusiasm, I took occasion to pronounce the obvious moral lesson, and tried to indicate to unhappy Beulah the similar injustice in her hatred of the Negro. Prejudice is always unfair, I pointed out, whether it be prejudice against the Okie or the man whose skin is black. She fairly shrieked in answer to my Christian counsels, "But I'm no nigger! I'm not black!" And, sobbing in her now immense distress, she ran off to tell whoever would listen that I had said she was "no better than a nigger wench."

Her complaints found fertile ground among her listeners, many of whom had no doubt been irked by my clumsy efforts to enlighten; no further incitement was needed to make me an object of persecution. My former lunchtime companions ostentatiously avoided me. I found signs red-lettered with the damning caption, "Nigger-lover," attached to my desk and chair. A newspaper clipping which described the lynching of a Florida Negro was left where it would surely come into my hands, with the penciled scrawl attached, "One of your pals, you ought to be with him." And at the same time, as I later learned, a petition was being circulated which requested my removal from the job and from this circle of my associates.

For a young and inexperienced person this was a violent introduction to the hatreds of the world. The trouble gradually died down, of course, and I was reabsorbed at last into the routine relationships of the group. Even Beulah forgot her indignation and became as friendly as ever. But to my eyes the broken pattern never quite seemed whole again, and try as I might I could not shake free from the horror of those few long days.

As a result of this experience I began to probe more deeply into the tangled undergrowth of race prejudice and to perceive how socially complex it was. Hatred of the Negro was no simple product of chance perversity on the part of the white shipyard worker. It was rather an indispensable constituent of his sense of well-being and the very foundation on which his estimate of his own importance was erected. His conviction that the Negro was inherently inferior carried with it the assurance of the white man's God-given right to the more prominent place in the sun. Thus even the most ignorant white shipyard worker whose post was at the bottom of a thousand higher steps might by virtue of racial heritage alone look arrogantly down upon his black-skinned companions in toil. I remember one old man who drifted through his days, avoiding conflict and choosing self-effacement, but who was decisive on the question of racial equalitarianism: "Well, a nigger may be as good as you are," he said, "but he sure ain't as good as me." This presumption of the black man's lesser status, which could give pride to the meek, was not to be abandoned without struggle. Little wonder, then, that anyone who threatened it, whether a rebel from the underlying group or a well-meaning rationalist like myself, was fought off more bitterly than a housebreaker or a pick-pocket; for that which rebel or rationalist would steal away was no mere thrifty sockful of cash, no mere hard-earned pay check, but <u>the defenses of the ego without which a man is poor indeed</u>.

The inferiority of the black man, as the white ship-yard worker conceived it, was all-pervasive and a fit subject for infinite argument and example. After the scorching wind of prejudice had passed by, the Negro was desiccated of every gift of nature, every trait of body or mind which might be commended. The mental inferiority of the race was complacently assumed in the shipyards; it was at the same time a subject of eager illustration. One native of Oklahoma, whose own school-ing had ended at the eighth grade, boasted that he could line up any hundred Negroes in the shipyard and prove that not twenty-five of them had reached the sixth grade, and that many could hardly write their own names. Nor was lack of opportunity primarily responsible; he as-sured me that it was a fundamental lack of ability, and then referred to the lack of skill and aptitude purport-edly displayed by Negro efforts in the trades. Tales which illustrated the Negro's incapacity in the crafts were in constant circulation, and it was commonly be-lieved by white workers that even the simplest mechan-ical processes were beyond his ability. I never heard a white man in the shipyard express himself as wholly satisfied with the workmanship of a Negro. Rare was the grudging admission, "Well, for a nigger, he's pretty good."

The concept of the <u>Negro's moral inferiority</u> was similarly implemented by stories and confirming arguments. When a crime was committed somewhere in the community, and when a tool was lost or a lunchbox stolen in the shipyard, the culprit was always imagined to possess black skin and frizzled hair. "You can't lay a thing down any more, with them niggers around," became the standard complaint of the worker who had temporarily misplaced a rule or a wrench. The moral shortcoming with which Negroes were most commonly taxed, however, was <u>laziness</u>, a trait which in the eyes of the self-respecting worker, whose roots were still deep in the soil of <u>Anglo-Saxon puritanism</u>, possessed a strong kinship with the devil and his nature. It was the consensus that a Negro worker waited only for the boss to disappear to slouch down into a corner and go peacefully to sleep. Even when compelled to stay awake, the Negro was asserted to be a master of the art of doing nothing busily. While observing the work of a gang of electricians which included a Negro member, I overheard one bystander make the caustic and typical remark, "Would you look at that lazy bastard of a nigger! Just hanging on the cable and pretending like he was really helping pull it." Another worker surmised that

laziness = immorality

the trait must have its origin in some disease which in
turn was the product of a deeper moral taint within the
race. "I think there must be something in nigger blood
that makes them lazy," he theorized; "maybe syphilis,
or something else that ain't got a name yet. Niggers are
so dirty anyway, I'll bet they have some kind of disease
that nobody else could have or ever heard of." In accordance with the peculiar taboos which governed shipyard conversation, especially in mixed company, sexual
diseases were seldom mentioned or discussed, but on
the few occasions when the word "syphilis" was spoken
in my presence, it was always in reference to a specific
Negro or the Negro group as a whole. The prevalence
of these diseases among the Negroes, furthermore (and
so far as shipyard opinion was concerned, all Negroes
were assumed to be diseased), was seen as the logical
consequence of their purported sexual looseness. The
lust of the Negro—and this was the culminating moral
indictment—was viewed as the lust of a wild animal and
considered to be as little subject to decent restraint.

The analogy between the Negro and the animal was
frequently used in shipyard argument. "Niggers, morally and in every other way, are beasts; get me?—just
beasts," was one man's summing up. The chain of theory
binding the Negro to the level of the animal was completely forged one afternoon when a shipyard worker
with whom I was riding home happened to observe a

passing Negro's unusual length of arm. "With those long arms," he chortled, "that nigger looks just like a chimpanzee"; and then he added as a serious after-thought, "They've found, you know, that apes and niggers are very close related."

The notion of Negro inferiority was not in itself sufficient basis for the white shipyard worker's hatred. Human beings often feel a particular affection toward those creatures—their dogs, for instance—which are inferior and confess their inferiority without reserve, and the Negro who keeps his proper place as bootblack or porter is typically not disliked; he may even be approved. But the Negro in America has long been restive in his inferiority. Further evidence of his determination to shake off the last remaining limitations of previous servitude was revealed in the course of the social dislocations consequent upon World War II. White workers in the shipyards, particularly those who had recently come from the South, did not need to look far to discover Negro encroachments upon what they had known as secure privilege. They soon realized that they were combatants on an active battlefield. They could feel the stirring of the Negro and his discontent beneath the very ground they walked on, and the impulses of emotionalism were, as a consequence, much more compelling for them than for persons removed from the conflict or comfortably exalted above it. With reason

these distressed and threatened people were alarmed
for the preservation of their precious sense of racial
status and the numerous social and economic advantages which attended it. With reason they reaffirmed
their faith in the native and ineradicable inferiority of
the Negro race. And granting their preconceptions,
granting the lives which they had lived and the teachings and traditions which were their heritage, it was
with reason likewise that they hated the black man and
his aspiring and multiplying spawn.

I wonder why

The ancient fear of despoliation of women of the
privileged race by men of inferior blood, which has
played so large a part in the establishment and elabora-
tion of caste systems in all societies, prevailed in the
shipyard as well. A rumor was almost always afloat of
some attempt by a Negro to satisfy his presumably constant sex hunger for the woman of white skin. There
were tales of surreptitious pinchings and maulings in
the secluded corners of the hulls, and of successful
sexual attacks in the dark streets of the Negro section
and in the housing units where Negroes and whites lived
in close proximity. I was never able to verify these accounts, but they were invariably accepted as factual
and worthy of repetition for their salacious interest and
inflammatory value. The Okies were especially disturbed and found it hard to accept the casual contact
between Negro men and white women to which North-

ern custom had long been indifferent—sitting together on streetcars and buses, standing together before lunch counters or pay windows, working side by side in the same gangs. Ordinary association enforced upon the two races by shipyard work and living was actively disapproved by those who were accustomed to rigid lines of separation, and open protests were occasionally made by an incensed individual. But for the most part the Okies were content to recount in bloody, brutal, and relished detail what remedies their home communities would prescribe for the Negro who went one step beyond the code. "Back where I come from," boasted one native of Missouri, "we've got a right and proper kind of home law, and if one of them black fellows even so much as talks smart to a white gal, we hang him dead." He recalled that on one occasion, some years before, a Negro boy had ventured to "talk smart" to a white schoolteacher of the town. "We tied that nigger to the schoolhouse roof," he continued with righteous emphasis, "and burned him to a crisp, schoolhouse and all. We didn't want none of the schoolhouse, and we didn't want none of the nigger, either. That's the way we feel about it in Missouri." Tales of lynchings with a background of sexual ravishment were much in demand, and in the savage sessions at which I was present no question, except my own perhaps, was ever raised against the propriety of lynching.

Few insults in shipyard parlance were more searing than "nigger-lover." A white man who sought the company of Negro women was exposed to scorn and partial ostracism. But the scorn was immeasurably multiplied when it was a white woman who desired or passively admitted the Negro's amorous attentions. With startling swiftness the anger of a race would gather and concentrate upon this one instance of desertion and betrayal. Just such fury spread over the hull on which I chanced to be at work one quiet afternoon when two young white girls, who were stringing cable next to a group of Negro machinists, chose to be as friendly with them as they would have been with a similar neighboring group of white boys. From mouth to mouth the story ran; probable objectors were hurried to the spot to observe for themselves and in turn to stoke the flames of indignation. Threats of public disgrace for the girls were becoming loudly vocal, and expressions of intent to expel them from the hull by force or to subject them to more memorable and brutal violence were crowding on the verge of positive action, when the decisive summons of the quitting whistle put a fortunate end both to the flirtation and to the clamor for punishment.

In the face of these attitudes no white woman, even if she wanted to, could establish normal friendly relations with a Negro man, or even talk with him at length on any topic. Contact of this type, no matter what its actual substance, was immediately translated by the on-looker into sexual terms. On the one occasion when I chanced to have a long and public conversation with a Negro man, the reaction of the shipyard audience was immediate and unequivocal. "Well, when's the wedding going to be?" a bystander inquired of me, and for days a trail of insinuation followed after the simple occurrence. White workers would admit no halfway point between the Negro's allotted role of servile, silent distance from the white woman and the intimacies of sexual union. Thus the entire issue of relationships between the races was enveloped in impenetrable obscurities of human impulse and emotionality, and could not be touched without evoking tribal cries against blood pollution.

[handwritten marginal note: She definitely sees this as pure irrationality]

Fear of the Negro was tangled with hatred and scorn of him. He was assumed to be inferior in mind, spirit, and body; but seldom did others venture to state the conviction in his presence. Indeed, vigorous Negro-baiting conversations sputtered into silence upon his unconcerned approach. Even the word "nigger" was not used in direct address, but was reserved for discourse within white sanctums. "A nigger don't like to be called a nigger to his face," a worker warned a younger and less cautious colleague; "if you call him that, he's as liable as not to pick up a piece of pipe and break your head with it."

As individuals, and as a group, Negroes were believed to be continually ready for aggression against the white man. Every Negro was reported to carry on his person a weapon, usually a razor or well-whetted knife, and it was rumored that arsenals were hidden in the Negro districts in preparation for an eventual major uprising. The imminence of violence was never far below the surface of shipyard anxieties. Any incident of interracial conflict might give rise to talk of rioting. One day soon after I went to work, a Negro woman was injured by an angry blow from a white man, and a nervous whisper was soon abroad that violent reprisal was planned. In the one fight between a white and a Negro which I witnessed—but I heard of several more—the distorted faces of the two principals who were rolling in the dust, the restlessness of the onlookers who quickly gathered, and the whole tension of the scene revealed the form of the race riot in horrid embryo. "If any trouble ever starts in this place," one white woman said, after seeing such a fight, "I'm going to jump in the bay and swim out as far as I can, because I know there will be killing, lots of killing."

Desire was added to fear in the white worker's contemplation of race rioting, for in self-sustained mob violence rather than individual challenge he found that solution to the problem of the Negro which most suited him. Physical repression, continually threatened and occasionally active, seemed to him the only means of keeping the Negro in his place. Many shipyard workers expressed satisfaction with the bloody Detroit race riots of 1943, and boasted of the greater carnage that would have taken place had they been there. One newcomer from the Southwest urged that a gun be issued to every white man in the Bay area as a measure of protection against the rising tide of Negro criminality and aggressiveness. "What you need round here," he further counseled, "is a good old-fashioned lynching. Back in my home state we string a nigger up or shoot him down, every now and then, and that way we keep the rest of them quiet and respectful."

The Negro, shipyard workers were acutely conscious, was not content with his place. He was relentlessly pushing upward, and it was the obvious burden of shipyard fear that he might not be satisfied with standing at the white man's side, but would push farther still to dominate his dominators. Southerners had especially dire predictions to make. The Negroes, they warned, would come in ever greater numbers to the lenient West; even after the war they would keep swarming to its cities to settle. They would crowd the white man from his homes, neighborhoods, places of social gathering and entertainment. "It's the niggers who are taking over California," an Okie remarked. "Pretty soon a white man in this state won't stand a chance." And persons whose smattering of knowledge was a little broader talked of the Negro's superior birthrate and of a coming annihilation beneath a surge of color. Once again a halfway point between complete degradation and complete triumph could not be found. To give an inch was to lose everything.

The extreme sensitivity of white workers to Negro presumptuousness was evident even in the rivalry for space on crowded buses and streetcars and priority at the shipyard exits so momentarily important at quitting time. A white man, caught and tossed and mauled in one of these mad scrambles, commonly emerged with the conviction that it was a Negro who had done the pushing from behind, a black fellow likewise who had blocked the way in front. One white worker angrily recounted to me an incident he had observed at quitting time on a recent afternoon: another white worker had been forced from his rightful place in the line of exit by the jostling and shoving of two Negro women. "By Jesus," he concluded, "I wouldn't let that happen to me. I'd sock those nigger wenches in the snoot before I'd let them push me out of line."

Negroes were also reputed, through roughness and the crude employment of their strength, to monopolize the seats and favored places on the streetcars. "Those niggers run to the streetcars like a bunch of stampeding cattle," complained a shipyard worker, "and a bunch of cattle is all they really are." <u>The very crushing together of black and white flesh in the enforced intimacies of public vehicles was an almost unbearable affront to fastidious members of the superior race.</u> Many shipyard workers went to some trouble to avoid the cars with routes serving unusually large numbers of Negroes. "I can't stand the smell of those niggers," a white worker said to me in explanation of his refusal to board a convenient and uncrowded car on which a number of Negroes were already riding. And in watching the thousands of private automobiles which streamed out of the yards at the end of the work shift I never once saw a white and a Negro worker sharing the same vehicle. With the close of the day and the emergence from the gates which marked the boundaries of control, the discipline of the shipyards was abruptly terminated, and in the wider outside area of free choice the white worker strove to dissociate himself sharply from his fellow toiler of the day whose skin was black, and thus, by avoidance of the visible offense, perhaps also to remove or at least allay the anxieties which the Negro aroused in him.

Aside from fear of the Negro as a sex rival and as a contender for place and prestige in society, a more overt and readily definable concern also motivated the white worker's hatred of the race; for the Negro in the shipyards was also an obvious and clamorous rival for

the all-important job and the weekly pay check which
were the bread and salt of life. Like women and Okies,
Negroes were trespassing on an exclusive domain where
skilled labor was well rewarded. It was, of course,
assumed by the white workers that Negroes, to a far
greater degree than other types of wartime newcomers,
were incapable of maintaining the standards of workmanship customary in the skilled trades. The sense of
injustice consequent upon the observation of Okies
and shipyard women and their presumably unearned
and undeserved position in the crafts was enormously
increased, therefore, with respect to the Negro who,
no matter how little or how poor his accomplishment,
received the same wages and was employed under
the same conditions as the skilled and diligent white
worker. Even more conducive to the white man's anxiety
and anger was the conviction, frequently emerging in
open statement, that the Negroes as a group were intent
upon eliminating the white worker from any economic
field where once they gained an entering foothold. In
spite of their lack of skill and their extraordinary back-
wardness, they were assumed to possess some mysterious but potent faculty of evil which would hasten their
triumph. Once again, should the Negro procure ever
so slight a share in the white man's world, he would
ultimately deprive its rightful owners of the whole. One
white worker believed that the catastrophe had already

occurred. It was—so he emotionally described the invasion of the shipyards—as if a mob of hoodlums had been let loose within a well-kept apple orchard, and in wanton disregard of the protests of the helpless husbandman were ravishing the fertility of the place and making it unfit for further use.

Some students of the Negro problem argue that economic rivalry fully explains all phenomena of racial antagonism. Certainly among the white man's fears which motivate his hatred of the Negro the fear of losing his economic security is the most logical and the most firmly founded on an indisputable threat; for, like any group whose living standards are low and who will work for low wages, Negroes have served, wherever present in large masses, to depress the white man's value on the labor market. Negroes and the poor whites of the South have long been pitted, one group against the other, in silent, deadly battle over the meager fruits of a grudging soil. In the Northern city whose industry but recently began to absorb them in significant numbers, Negroes had no loyalties to the cause of labor, and already had often been employed as strikebreakers to smash the white man's unions and forestall his just demands for better working conditions. Knowing such facts as these, the white worker who looked no deeper than the surface could easily find ample reasons for his fear and hatred of the Negro.

In their role as agencies of job protection and monopoly, American trade unions did valiant battle against extension of the field of Negro employment. Many international and national labor organizations affiliated with the American Federation of Labor barred Negroes from membership by constitutional provision; others accomplished the same purpose by devious techniques; still others segregated Negroes into auxiliaries with restricted powers. Until the emergence of the Committee for Industrial Organization, with its conscious opposition to racial discrimination, it was a rare union that invited Negroes to share freely in the advantages of membership. Thus, most Negroes worked outside the protection of labor organizations and were everywhere generally restrained to casual and ill-paid industrial work, whence, however, they could the more readily be drawn to act as strikebreakers and subverters of the white man's living standards.

The shipbuilding unions of the Bay Area stood almost solidly with the national example in barring Negroes, and, since closed-shop agreements were customary in the region, exclusion of the Negro from the unions was tantamount to his exclusion from all participation in the skilled trades. Before the outbreak of the war, Negroes had no place in Bay Area shipyard work. But the declaration of hostilities in 1941 brought union policies of racial exclusion, in the shipyards as in all other types of war industry, into sharp conflict with the need to exploit all resources of man power in spite of conventional niceties.

Even in the face of this demand only two of the large unions at Moore Dry Dock—the C.I.O. Machinists' Union (the only C.I.O. union) and the A. F. of L. Laborers' Union, the second of which was expressly organized to absorb the wartime swarm of unskilled shipyard maintenance men—welcomed the Negro without delay to full status as a member. Other unions offered more or less resistance to Negroes, and only accepted them when the arguments of management and the directives of government agencies demonstrated that the inescapable alternative was loss of the closed shop. These unions which under duress grudgingly removed the barriers to Negro membership usually did so with reservations calculated to hasten a return to exclusiveness when the demands of war should slacken. The Boilermakers' Union, for example, confined Negroes to an auxiliary which could not vote. A few unions succeeded in maintaining an entirely closed door. The Teamsters' Union was one; another was the Steamfitters' Union, which was the heir of a decades-long and nation-wide history of successful resistance to Negro demands for entrance. Both of these unions, incidentally, had a large wartime membership of women, whom they had accepted, it would seem, in lieu of Negroes. The Steamfitters' Union, furthermore, continued to deny admission to the Negro in spite of progressive local leaders who would have defied national headquarters, and the rank and file as well, had they been confident of accomplishing thereby more than their own immediate destruction.

Union officials, in excluding Negroes from their organizations or limiting the privileges of those who did get in, pursued a course applauded by most of their white membership. I have witnessed in the meetings of my own union the furor which arose at the slightest hint of relaxation of official barriers. "The officers of this union can do what they want about a lot of things, so far as I'm concerned," one member announced in open meeting; "they can spend all the money in the treasury, suspend the constitution, declare themselves permanently elected, and I won't raise a stink. But I sure will be here shouting if they try to let those niggers in. It's all I ask of them—that they keep those black boys out." In such outbursts no effort was made to analyze the basis for excluding the Negro. No one said, "The labor market may shrink and we shouldn't admit, just for now, a whole new group that could compete with us later." However important economics may be in the maintenance of race prejudice, I never heard, either at union meetings or in the shipyard, a developed statement of resistance to the Negro on the basis of the threat to job security which he represented. Rather, these economic arguments against race equality were reduced to the emotional level of distaste for social, and ultimately sexual, contact with the Negro. Whether consciously or not, anxieties of economics were brought as close as possible to the question, "Do you want your daughter to marry a nigger?"—the reply to which was automatic and required no justifying. The emotion which dominated resistance to the sharing of union privileges, and the entire issue of equal economic opportunity, was the emotion which resisted the intermingling of the races on the streetcars or sexual converse between them. Negroes were assumed to be as rightfully excluded from the white man's union and jobs as from his neighborhood and social gatherings.

Admission of the Negro to a union, when finally it was gained, did not, of course, allow free access to the opportunities of the trade. On the job, the Negro was still subject to discriminatory practices. His were the less-favored, arduous tasks. "That's nigger work," a white boss would remark; "a white man shouldn't have to do it," and wherever arrangements could be made to that end, it was the Negro whose strength was called upon to accomplish the unpleasant chore. Desirable work with premium pay was effectively held beyond his grasp. Pipe welding, for instance, demanded greater skill and paid more than ordinary plate welding, but

Negroes, although many of them became efficient welders, were almost entirely excluded from it. "I don't want any niggers for this job," a supervisor of pipe welders told his leaderman on despatching him for replacements. "Take Okies or women if you can't find anything better, but don't bring back no niggers."

Advancement, likewise, was difficult for Negroes. Many did obtain a journeyman's status and rate of pay in the crafts in which they were well represented, but I knew of no Negro who became a supervisor except among laborers and riggers, where all-Negro gangs were occasionally formed with a Negro straw boss. The typical white worker preferred death, he would assert for the sake of emphasis, to working under a Negro. In defense of the white workers in the Philadelphia streetcar strike of 1944 an irate pipefitter declared: "The employers have only themselves to blame when they try to make foremen out of a bunch of niggers and people get mad and go on strike. I sure would do the same myself. If they put a nigger foreman over me in the shipyards, patriotism could go to hell; I'd quit on the spot."

The shipyard structure of racial prejudice had innumerable consequences of discrimination and antagonism in the practical, day-to-day relationships between Negro and white worker, and yet it was itself amazingly impervious to the world of fact and influence. It was rather like a Platonic form—with beginnings that were beyond search and validity that was beyond question. For the white workers of the shipyard, full though they were of talk concerning the nature, capacities, and intentions of the Negro, did not know the Negro as he was and did not desire to know him. In fact, the very force of their prejudice was calculated to maintain a distance between black and white, across which any but the most casual and formalized contact was impossible. "A white guy just naturally don't want to associate with niggers," one man explained; "he don't want to talk with them, eat with them, or walk along the same side of the street where they are." Therefore the Negroes whom the white worker saw day after day in the course of his shipyard toil never became a group of friends or even of individuals having temperaments as various as their names, but eternally remained stereotyped, their characteristics prefabricated by the observer's prejudice. The Negro, who was despised and hated in the shipyards, was even more of a symbol than the Okie, who was good-naturedly ridiculed; and the actual Negro, furthermore, unlike the actual Okie—the white native of the rural Southwest,—was not able to emerge from this caricature of himself into the realm of the accepted and individualized, for, whatever his other triumphs of adjustment to the patterns of the dominant group, he could never change the color of his skin.

The Negroes made little effort as a group to rebel against their segregation or to revise the shape and content of the white man's prejudice against them. Convinced, doubtless, of the futility of resistance, they kept to themselves for the most part, ate in separate parties, had their private jokes, and maintained an air of indifference to the world from which they were excluded. Negro women in particular were difficult to approach even when familiarity was encouraged. They shrank to the end of lunchtime queues, limited conversation with a white worker to answering in monosyllables, and seemed in every timid gesture willingly to acknowledge their own inferiority. Indeed, the entire behavior of the shipyard Negroes, as I saw it, provided pitifully little foundation for fears of the black man's aggressiveness.

Exceptional Negroes, of course, so far resented the conventions as to discard all pretense of accepting them. These were the "uppity niggers" and "sassy black fellows" about whom the white workers especially complained. Some of the more flagrant examples of the type may actually have been, as reputed, recent arrivals from the South for whom the new partial freedom was too sudden. But whatever their origins or their motivations, certain Negroes in the shipyards made advances toward white women, shouldered their powerful way to the front through shocked but yielding crowds, or outcursed and outbrazened the white boss to become

at length embroiled, as if it were the climax they were
seeking, in a violent physical encounter with some
champion of the affronted clan.

Aggressiveness was not invariably displayed, however, in such undisciplined acts. Occasionally the same
defiance of discriminatory custom was channeled into
a conscious effort by a Negro to explain himself and his
people, and to demand redress of grievances. The only
contacts of any depth or permanence which I succeeded
in establishing across the barrier of race were with two
Negroes, one a woman and one a man, who were admittedly and openly rebellious. Their ideologies, as it
happened, were representative of the two broad schools
of recent Negro reformist thought. One school, orig-
inating in the cautious teachings of Booker T. Washington, sought no more than equal opportunity within
a context of continuing segregation. The later school,
finding its official mouthpiece in the National Association for the Advancement of Colored People, demanded a radical restatement of the status of the Negro
and an end to almost all educational, economic, and
social barriers.

The woman whose philosophy embodied the teachings of the former school was a mulatto, attractive
and dignified. Through education and careful self-
improvement she had achieved an individual triumph,
she maintained, which sufficed for her. Since other

Negroes might follow the course she had taken, this program of quiet growth and studied cultivation should, she felt, eventually prove sufficient for the race. Her father, a successful Texas farmer, was addressed by the title "Mister," she proudly pointed out, by all the white storekeepers with whom he traded. She herself had taught school in her home state, and was also trained in the various skills of office work. The office job which she had sought at Moore Dry Dock had been refused her, "because of my race, of course," but in her position as matron of a woman's rest room—"they told me it was all that was available at the time"—she bore herself with the dignity of a duchess at her tea table. Her revolt against the world of prejudice, which had denied her the fulfillment of her capacities, was sublimated into a conscious condescension, a sense of being above the torment and the tormentors. Even in the trying spring of 1943, with its outbursts of race rioting throughout the country and its sympathetic tension in the shipyards, she continued calm and gracious; she doubted, she said to me, that any further trouble would occur, and if it did she was confident that her people could meet it and achieve victory in the end. "Why, you know," she stated almost smugly, "an average Negro man is a match for any three of these white weaklings in the shipyard," and in the mere assertion of the ability of her race she found the remedy for all the injustice. The inward substance

of equality was hers; the outward form might happily
be ignored.

The man, small, very dark, tense and keen, had no
such haven. The aimless rebellions of his childhood and
youth had at last found a course—in the broad stream
of revolutionary reform. With amazing skill, consider-
ing the intensity of his purpose and the unpopularity
of his cause, he maintained good relations with his fellow workers, both black and white, while he preached
a doctrine of change which, he argued, would prove of
ultimate benefit to all Americans. He was a fanatic and
a monomaniac, whose sole topic of conversation was
the crying injustice under which his people suffered;
his every nerve was stretched to twanging tautness by
the strength of his zeal. Beads of perspiration started
from his forehead while he spoke, and his eyes were
in restless search of further converts. Yet it was only
through him and others like him that the discontent of
a silent people had vocal substance; such rare rebels'
demands, whether granted or refused, could not be
ignored.

The Negroes at Moore Dry Dock were not altogether
deprived of a bar of relatively impartial justice to which
to bring their problems of adjustment. In the first place,
the management of the yards, having been compelled
to hire thousands of Negroes, was interested in obtaining some value from its investment. Amicable relation-

ships between white and black workers were therefore encouraged, sporadically, by articles in the shipyard weekly newspaper praising the work of outstanding Negro employees, by display of government posters urging coöperation between the races, and on one occasion by the choice of an all-Negro group to launch a ship, in token, it was said, of the contribution which Negroes in the armed services and in defense industries had made toward the winning of victory.

The management, however, displayed no deep or consistent sympathy, and the efforts which were dutifully made were counterbalanced by occasional outbursts of antagonism, which grew and reproduced themselves in the receptive soil of the shipyards far more vigorously than the conciliatory words and moral preachments. One member of the shipyard's governing family made a public statement, printed in the local press, to the effect that he was disappointed with the incapacity and indolence of his Negro workers. The few who had read the statement repeated it to those who had not, and it was soon common gossip in the yards, a magnified and satisfying substantiation of already existent opinion. At another time, a bulletin, ostensibly intended only for Negro workers and chiding them as a class for their alleged small purchases of war bonds, was issued at the gates at quitting time. It fell inevitably into the curious hands of all who passed. One white shipyard worker, who to my certain knowledge had never himself bought a war bond, carried the bulletin about with him for days and read it aloud to all who were not familiar with its content, which to him plainly gave managerial sanction to his prejudice.

Fortunately, the Negro might appeal his claims to still more powerful and less partial agencies than the management. For, like a vast, exalted sky, the government and the law extended over a whole land of racial conflicts. Groups of militant Negroes and a scattering of white collaborators made resolute use of the instrumentalities of change which the law provided, especially in combating union policies which excluded Negroes or segregated them in auxiliaries. In spite of a general indifference to governmental activities, reverberations of these legal disputes were occasionally heard in the shipyards. A decision by a local judge unfavorable to the Negroes' case against the Boilermakers' Union aroused the rejoicing of several of my colleagues. Government intervention in the Philadelphia streetcar strike, on the other hand, was met with sarcasm and resistance by the same colleagues. "Who is the government, anyway?" one of them said. "It's you and me; and if we don't want to associate with niggers and let them into our unions, why, the government sure ain't going to make us do it." On the whole, however, the appeals by Negroes and their frequent victories unquestionably gave them status as a people in the eyes of their white companions in toil. Mutterings might result when courts decided in favor of the Negroes, but the decision was respected, and the conviction grew that the law, at least—if not quite the intangible and sacred quality of justice,—was on the side of the black man and his sorrows.

The unions of the shipyards played a conservative, not to say reactionary, role in obstructing the Negro's entrance into the industrial field. Even unions with no avowed restrictions upon Negro membership made no serious effort to improve interracial relationships, either within their own organizations or in the social world at large. But here too the Negro was not entirely lacking in his champions, for numbers of union members and officers, who were what one among them called "right-thinking people," sought strenuously to end racial discrimination in trade-union democracy as a first step toward ending it in American democracy as a whole. Men of this mind eventually led the union to which I belonged. I was present at one memorable meeting held under their guidance at which—save for the outburst of one extremely prejudiced person—the question of Negro membership was discussed with calmness, as if it were an ordinary problem of union policy. The influence of these men was not enough, during wartime at least, to alter the prearranged program of the unions, but their existence was indirectly indicated both in occasional articles decrying racial prejudice which appeared in the trade-union press and in the support which many unions gave to community-wide efforts at reform. A labor school in the Bay Area, for instance, a school expressly founded to serve the needs of working people and emphasizing in its curriculum the minority and race problems of America, depended for a great part of its support upon contributions from the unions, the Steamfitters' among them. One member of this union visited the school out of curiosity and came back to tell an open meeting that Negro men and white women sat side by side in the classrooms and danced together at its parties. "Is that what we're paying a hundred bucks a month to see?" he demanded. "A bunch of niggers with their arms around white women?" But in spite of his protest the stipend was continued. To that degree the "right-thinking people" were able to prevail even in a union which excluded Negroes.

The shipyard situation itself, in the final analysis, and the disturbing, altering influences which it exerted upon accustomed patterns of behavior, superseded in strength and compulsion all consciously directed agencies of reform. Changelessness in attitudes and conduct, where relations between Negro and white workers were concerned, should not be emphasized, moreover, to the total exclusion of change. For change there obviously was. Its variety and degree appear as especially note-worthy when the Okies are considered. Most, if not all, of these people had never used the same toilet facilities or eaten at the same tables or sat in the same streetcar seats with a Negro until they migrated to the shipyards. They would have judged such familiarity unbearable. Yet from their first day in the shipyards they accepted it without open revolt, and after a few months even their protests tended to die away.

The white worker who was native to the area or who came from a Northern state had his own measure of adjustment to make; he was unaccustomed to working in an industry where so many Negroes were congre-gated, some having a status and a pay check equal to his own. Although his initial resistance to the social contact was not so great as that of the Southern white, he was keenly aware of the Negro's threat to his job security; such of the other aspects of race antagonism as he did not already have, he tended quickly to acquire. In fact, except for the greater emotionality of the Southerner, and his more frequent talk of lynchings, riots, and re-prisals, the attitudes of the two groups were hard to dis-tinguish. Nevertheless, within the shipyard and beneath its discipline, which was like that of the schoolroom and the church in its power to command, Southern white and Northern white, repressing their impulse to revolt, worked with the Negro.

In my two years of searching at Moore Dry Dock, I found only one white worker—a woman—who declared that she felt no prejudice against the Negro and was eager to see the end of all racial discrimination in America. She was a Californian by birth, a woman of great good heart and superior education, and she had an altogether engaging way with those large numbers of shipyard workers who disagreed with her. "My boy," she said in motherly fashion to one young chap who had launched full tilt into a violent anti-Negro tirade, "My boy, you have so very much to learn"; and by the manner, if not the content, of her remark she knocked the wind out of him for the time.

Even aside from this one bright exception, however, shipyard prejudice against the Negro was not all of one piece. There were those, for instance, who ventured to express affection, or at least tolerance, for the Negro who knew how to keep his place. "It's them sassy niggers I don't like," one remarked to me. "If it weren't for them I wouldn't mind the niggers much at all." Or distinctions in disapproval and approval might be made between the Southern and the Northern Negro, some preferring the former "because he knows how a nigger ought to act to a white man," and some the latter because he had more of the graces of the white man's civilization. One observer of more serious type, who had lived both in the North and in the South and who was himself comparatively well-read, asserted that although he did not like the Negroes and tried to avoid close contact with them he felt that it was not to innate stupidity but to lack of opportunity that their inadequacies were due. "I know a Negro welder in the yards," he told me, employing the rare word "Negro" hesitantly, "who's been to college and talks just like a white man. You wouldn't want a better worker than he is." He mentioned another educated Negro and that Negro's contempt for the less-favored members of his race. "It's education makes the difference," he concluded. "You can't change the color of a black man's skin, and there are other things about him you can't change either, but if you send him to school for a long enough time you can sure make him a lot easier to work around."

Shipyard prejudice varied, too, in the degree of proximity between the races which it would countenance in different realms of human contact. Sexual and social converse—the possible relationships of lovers, friends, or neighbors—lay beyond the borders of acceptance and was automatically and indignantly rejected, owing to fear which was too deep for logical analysis and too strong to need a justifying argument. But another type of contact was not so universally proscribed. I came upon several shipyard workers who declared their unqualified support of the Negro's right to work beside the white man, earn the same pay, and have the same opportuni-

ties for economic advancement—remarks which I found
particularly interesting since the economic rivalry between black worker and white has loomed so large in
the problems of interracial relationships. Ample evidence has shown that the white worker feared the competition of the Negro, and yet, in this area of tension
as nowhere else, abstract concepts of justice appeared
to have most power over the naked impulses of selfishness. "A nigger has a right to earn a living for himself
and his family like anybody else," one shipyard worker
said. "If niggers are good workers and want to work,"
another admitted, "I guess we can't keep hold of all the
jobs." One worker analyzed his own reactions to the situation with extraordinary clarity. He hated and despised Negroes, he explained, with whom he could not
bear to associate where freedom of choice was his, but
he knew that the trend of the times was against any wish
he might cherish to exclude them from fuller economic
opportunity, and in all justice he had to allow the validity of their claim.

It is difficult to estimate how much these various
attitudes of tolerance were increased by the years of
enforced association in the shipyard. The discipline of
the shipyard, forceful though it was, was able directly
to influence external conduct only; it had no technique
for quenching the resentment which still smoldered
even after the flame had been extinguished or brought

under control; for if any one man, with his full-grown complement of tangled suspicions and insecurities, cannot quickly broaden his mind, how much less can some thousands of shipyard workers be persuaded to relinquish their ancient dogmas and fetishes by two or three years of living part-time under an alien code? The glories of sudden conversion were here beyond the reach of the most sanguine hope. Moreover, the compulsions of the shipyards, while lessening some of the discrimination, also increased the tensions of resistance among those who were forced to conform. It was therefore possible that this brief experience of conflict, rather than weakening old attitudes, may have emphasized them yet more. For most white workers, certainly, hatred of the Negro remained, at the end of their shipyard years, what it had been at the beginning, a precious component of their system of personal security. Although a few outer forms of tolerance had been readily achieved, the creation of inner conviction waited upon further time and much further guidance.

Over the period of the Negro's slow advance from slavery, however, no important eminence has been captured to be relinquished later. The Negroes who moved northward during World War I remained in the less-bigoted environment, and the few outposts of livelihood beyond the lines of menial service which they held in the time of acute need for man power were for the most part retained. So it seems safe to venture that the Negroes who went north and west in World War II will settle where they traveled, and will continue to be considerable factors in the industrial life of their communities. The white worker in heavy industry and the skilled trades may still come to the table first and take the best seat; but now the Negro sits there, too.

LESSER MINORITIES

⚜️ THE NEGRO was at the bottom of the white shipyard worker's order of races, and the man of Teutonic, Scandinavian, or Anglo-Saxon stock—the unequivocal white man—was at the top. Various gradations of peoples in between were disapproved by the dominant group in accordance with their distance below it. No carefully enunciated philosophy of Nordic or Anglo-Saxon supremacy was included in this conception; it was a matter simply of the vague and comfortable belief that to be able to trace one's ancestry back to the favored western regions of Europe was to be at the peak of racial endowment, from which it was possible to view with superiority and scorn the mass of darker-skinned humanity below.

These lesser groups included even such Americans as those whose family origins were in the Slavic and Latin countries of Europe. One shipyard worker to whom I spoke, a man particularly interested in the details of race distinction, limited the white race strictly to those peoples whose eyes were blue and whose hair was light brown or preferably blond. He argued vehemently that White Russia was so named because it was the only area in Russia in which the people were really white. "Most Russians I've ever seen," he said in support of his contention, "have had black hair and dark skin, and you could tell by looking at them that they were a mixture of the Lord only knows what breeds." He also eliminated the Irish from the charmed circle of the blond-haired race: they were a folk whose purity of blood had been adulterated as a result of hospitality to Moors cast on Ireland's shore from the wreck of the Spanish Armada. Extreme though his theory of racial purity was, it was but slightly better documented and developed than the dogma cherished by many others in the yards.

Among the peoples occupying intermediate positions in the order of races, the Portuguese, of whom there were many in the shipyards and surrounding communities, were held in especial contempt. Their place, indeed, was second in lowliness only to that of the Negroes; detractors would often point to superficial likenesses in the two groups—for instance, the taste for flashy dress—which indicated, it was argued, a close affinity in blood. "Those Portygees are only streamlined niggers anyway," one commentator summed them up. "Look at the way they throw their money around on diamond rings and big, shiny cars. Why, they haven't any more brains than a nigger's got." The Portuguese, for all their asserted inferiority, were not limited by the studied discrimination which surrounded the Negroes, and several of them achieved positions of responsibility in the crafts of ship construction. But it was the general conviction that they then became, with their small minds and affection for display, power-mad and tyrannical bosses. "Make a Portygee a leaderman," said one worker, "and he tries to act like Mussolini." Yet this prejudice was not so firmly founded that an individual might not, by intelligence and tact, upset it. I knew one Portuguese, a foreman of the plumbers, who, obviously on the defensive because his name and origin were counted against him, was loud-mouthed, bullying, and totally lacking in dignity. He was commonly disliked and ridiculed and never dissociated from the scornful term, "Portygee." But another Portuguese, who also held a job of some authority but whose manner was gentle and unfailingly good-humored, was accepted and well spoken of, and the darkness of his skin was casually dismissed by reference to a touch of "Spanish blood."

The shipyard attitude toward Mongolian peoples was complicated by the Pacific war and by old antagonisms. California's history of anti-Oriental agitation is long and full of ugly incident, and much of it has welled from working-class hatreds. Again, concern for wage standards and job monopolies was important in the agitation, and labor unions in the State actively supported restriction of Oriental immigration as well as discriminatory practices against those Chinese, Japanese, and Filipinos already residing in the country. So far as attitudes toward the Japanese were concerned,

whether these Japanese were inhabitants of the aggressive Empire itself or American-born, the Pacific war
was merely another chapter in a lengthy story of antagonism. Workers who were long-time residents of
California were well seasoned in their detestation of
the people, while others, although they might never
have seen a Japanese, soon acquired the fashionable
hate—so universal and passionate a hate that, had an
unprotected Japanese been suddenly released within
the shipyard, he would, I have no doubt, have been in
danger of physical affront, perhaps even death. The
principal purpose of the war, to most shipyard workers,
was to hunt down these monsters in human form and
exterminate them. In coat lapels appeared buttons with
"Registered Jap Hunter" or "Open Season on Japs,"
and audiences welcomed tales of tortures that were
perpetrated on "them yellow-bellied bastards" by the
stalwart American soldier or marine. "If I was young
enough to fight this war," a worker well past the draft
age declared, "you wouldn't catch me being nice to the
Nips and taking any prisoners. I'd kill 'em all and kill
'em good and slow."

All Japanese had been evacuated from coastal California by the time I assumed my shipyard post, and
some liberals had begun to urge that the constitutional
rights of Japanese-Americans be considered fairly and
to hint that their former homes be returned to those

whose loyalty was proved. Shipyard resistance to such suggestions was immediate. Placards on windshields announced the intention to "Keep the Japs Out." Especially incensed persons openly threatened to take measures of vengeance into their own hands should the Japanese be allowed to come back. No Jap could possibly be loyal to America. Tales were circulated of the prewar machinations of the Black Dragon Society in California's Little Tokyos, as were all the well-known rumors of sabotage on and after December 7. "A Jap is a Jap, whether he was born in California or Timbuctoo," one worker assured me. "I've worked with them and done business with them for years, and I know there's not one of the yellowbellies you can trust."

Chinese, either as a people or as individuals employed in the yards, were accepted without resistance or dislike, though with little positive friendliness. I recall no comment on them, except one statement which contrasted Chinese honesty with Japanese dishonesty and trickiness. Their isolation from the hurly-burly at Moore Dry Dock was furthered by their own extreme reserve and by their concentration in electrical work—supervised by a Chinese. On the whole, Mongolians, whether Japanese or Chinese, were not judged according to quite the same scale of values as other minorities, whose wholesale inadequacies marked them out for hatred or contempt. The Mongol, mysterious, untrustworthy, often ruthless, but too clever to be despised, stood somewhat apart from the hierarchy of scorn, although he was still assumed to be, in a moral sense at least, an inferior of the white man.

By some sophistry one type of Mongolian, the American Indian, was released from the heavy yoke of shipyard disapproval. The few full-blooded Indians who worked in the yards were respected, liked, and even admired by their white brethren. One Navajo, a skilled silversmith, carried on with a large circle of friendly and more-than-friendly shipyard women a flourishing business in silver-and-turquoise trinkets. The Okies, furthermore, the Negro-hating, Jap-abhorring Okies, were invariably proud of any trace of Cherokee blood which they might claim. Even enlightenment on the Mongolian affinities of the Indian (which I maliciously provided) never seemed to trouble their complacency or to moderate the noisy advertisement of their mixed ancestry. Thus, a crowning triumph of confusion and illogicality, the minority groups which were most valued and most hated were both of the same race.

Logic and fact were of little moment in shaping and maintaining shipyard views on race. Obvious in each shipyard attitude thus far discussed has been the dominance of preconception over experience, the triumph of the traditional type over the individual exception. The infinite variety of fact was always tortured to fit the narrow pattern of a prejudice. But the most flagrant employment of this process yet awaits consideration; for to a degree beyond that of any other racial opinion the shipyard concept of the Jew was manufactured from stale convention and groundless prejudice.

Jews, as it happened, were rare in the shipyard, and even tended to conceal their identities behind the less damning labels of Italian or Spanish or Greek, a concealment simplified by the shipyard worker's picture of the Jewish physical type. The only avowed Jews with whom he commonly had personal contact were the penny-grabbing petty merchant, the keeper of the secondhand clothes shop, the junk buyer, and the proprietor of the corner delicatessen—tradesmen serving only to reinforce the legend of Jewish avarice which had descended unmodified from the Middle Ages. One man, whenever he discussed Jews, unfailingly trotted forth a detailed account of an unprofitable experience of his own with a Jewish junk dealer. "Just like all the Jews, that sheeny was," he habitually concluded. "He wore a little round black cap, and he couldn't speak the English, but he sure knew how to cheat a workingman out of his last, hard-earned dime." It was commonly believed in the shipyards that Jews played no part in accomplishing the useful work of the world. They were said to be front-office men entirely, who never soiled their hands with the grease of industry or the manure of a farm. "I've never seen or heard of a Jew who did an honest day's work in my life," said a skilled craftsman with a high regard for the products of manual toil. "They all know too well how to fatten on the sweat of other men."

Jews were unique among the disapproved minorities of the shipyards in being credited with certain qualities which were superior, rather than inferior, to those with which the ordinary run of humankind are gifted. "Jews are cleverer than us white men are; they're cleverer than anybody else on earth," was the emphatic and unchallenged remark of one shipyard worker. It was this very cleverness, in fact, this willingly conceded superiority, that was resented most bitterly, since it was the basis on which the reputed power and wealth of the Jew were presumed to rest. The Jew further infuriated common workingmen because he was reported to hold the fortress of his own exclusiveness against all comers. Bits of gossip concerning Jewish custom were scattered through the shipyards, and much point was made of the notion that a Jewish family went into mourning as for one dead if a son or daughter so far forgot the honor of his race as to marry outside the clan. "To a Jew, a non-Jew is like dirt," explained a shipyard "authority," and those who heard him hold forth on the topic of Jewish contempt for the Gentile were as angered by the insult as if the Jew himself had spat upon them.

Little of a religious tone existed in the shipyard attitude toward the Jew. Occasionally, as a corroborating argument, reference would be made to the "fact" that the Jews showed their colors early by "killing Christ." But the principal issues were economic and social. "Jew" was the readiest word at hand for summing up the villainy of any man of wealth and influence whose power was envied and whose activities were disapproved. According to some, Franklin Roosevelt was a Jew, and in the 1944 election campaign one Roosevelt supporter felt it necessary to request refutation of this slander from an official source and to carry the answering letter about with him. Notable men of wealth, such as the Morgans, the Rockefellers, and the Vanderbilts, were also alleged to be of Jewish stock; however, an Italian lad, whose Judophobia was extreme, excepted Henry Ford from this infamous company, "because he shares his money with the poor." A few so far disregarded logic as to mark Hitler with the Jewish brand. It was common talk that the war was caused by Jews, and that Moore Dry Dock was itself controlled by Jewish capital. "If you want to get anywhere in this shipyard," I was solemnly assured by several persons, "you've got to kiss the feet of Meester Nat Leevy first" (the name was conventionally distorted by the shipyard concept of a Yiddish dialect), "for he's the guy who really owns the company."

Jews, in the shipyard view, were loan sharks, shyster lawyers, union-breakers, capitalists, and everything in capitalism that was destructive of the welfare of the common man. The San Francisco Woman Shoppers' League, having helped to smash a retail clerks' strike which had been the pet of a union-conscious worker, was, in his view, composed of "Jew bitches." Another man asserted that the directing council of the Bank of America, which had foreclosed his farm in central California, was also exclusively Jewish. As the shipyard group conceived them, all Jews were grinders of the faces of the poor, the Lord and Lady Moneybags who grew rich upon a worker's toil and burgeoned on the flesh and blood of his children. They were the crooked gamblers of the land, embezzlers, grafting politicians; they were a people utterly lacking in scruple, who coiled serpent-like round the heap of their ill-gotten gains and destroyed all who challenged their possession.

The ills of the world were almost entirely the product of Jewish trickery. Time and again I have heard the statement that, whatever crimes Hitler had committed, his ruthless pursuit of the Jewish evil was praiseworthy and in the best interests of the Christian world. "You got to hand it to Hitler for taking the money away from the Jews the way he did," one worker said; "somebody ought to do the same thing in America."

THE PATTERN OF STATUS

✻ RACIAL TERMS and categories were the common coinage of the shipyard worker's social intercourse, and he felt most confident in his likes and dislikes, whether on the individual or the group level, when he could reduce them to the fundamental biological denominator of the inborn and racially determined. That any unpopular, inadequate, or unprincipled man was also the member of a disapproved race was a discovery eagerly made and publicized, for therein was contained at once the definition and explanation of the evil and the opprobrium which befitted it. So strong was the tendency thus to classify all differences between men that even the Okies were frequently considered as the product not of a peculiar environment but of a long line of blood inheritance.

This type of thinking had many advantages for those who tended to be impatient with the complexity of fact. Clear boundaries could be drawn between the world of the alien and the world of one's own people. Troublesome shadings were avoided and equivocation was put aside. Either an individual belonged to a given group or he did not, and his affiliation was fixed by birth. For those who could identify themselves with the Anglo-Saxon and Teutonic elite, the system had much of Calvinism's wonderful attraction for the Calvinist. Since nature and nature's God had chosen to mark off the sheep from the goats in the human family with brands of race, the chosen, white-skinned few were left to en-joy the sense of their election without concern for lesser breeds and their miseries. The concept could be further simplified by reducing the confusing multitudes of the alien to a series of homogeneous types having character-istics of tradition rather than of experience. Collections of traits were made into uniforms which were cut to conceal all differences of stature within a group. The uniform, indeed, came often to have a life and vigor of its own entirely apart from the body which was to fill it. In the Jew this triumph of the uniform was complete, and a race was conceived and given breath from the unsanctified alliance of prejudice and imagination.

The various minority groups in the shipyards, the groups against whom attitudes of antagonism were cher-ished or policies of discrimination maintained, were with one exception racial or pseudoracial units. Women alone stood outside the categories of race, though the characteristics which made them unfit for the type of work they were trying to do in heavy industry were assumed to be innate and biologically determined, and raised therefore a similarly fixed barrier to coöperative contact. All these groups were bound, moreover, by uniformities in the reactions which they aroused, by uniformities in the whole structure of prejudice and policy which was built around them. Whether the minority in question was composed of women, Jews, Okies, or Negroes, much of what might be said concerning one of them and the nature of its isolated and precarious position in the shipyard social system would hold for any other, or for them all. These several companies of people were not reduced, of course, to a common level of value. Rather they were dispersed along a loose and often self-contradictory scale of better and worse, the topmost place on which was occupied by the arbiting elite.

Almost all minorities, then, were debited with a general inferiority of endowment, of which their social ineffectiveness and economic dependence were adequate testimony. The degree of this inferiority varied, however. Negroes were at the bottom of the scale, practically akin to beasts. Women's inferiorities, though constantly limiting factors in the entire field of their activities, were only emphasized in the context of the economic rivalry with men. Some Okies, though belonging to an inferior class, could improve and eventually be accepted within the circle of the dominant group. But whatever the inferiority quotient might be, nature having decided it, society affirmed it with appropriate lack of riches, prestige, and position.

Only the Jew stood apart from this just and logical plan and served to mar the harmonious linkage of natural and social judgment; for although, in the shipyard view, the Jew was racially inferior to the Gentile, his cleverness, arrogance, deceit, and greed had made him the undeserving master of power and wealth. In contradiction to righteous principle, the magnitude of his sins was matched, not by failure, but by the magnitude of his success. The shipyard worker, for once unable to look complacently down upon an inferior people toiling at an inferior level in society, felt himself compelled to look up. While he despised the group, he coveted what it owned.

The highest rung on the shipyard ladder, the position of the industrially experienced Yankee, was sanctified by tradition and confirmed by the decrees of nature; but it was not a perch of unqualified security. The Jew had negated much of its rightful superiority, and even those groups whose status was as low as their supposed capacities were obviously growing restless on the lower rungs and were pushing upward. The fears of the elite were multiplied by the fact of minority intrusion into the hitherto protected area of the shipyard. Resentment and fear of further presumption bred the hatred and suspicion which dominated intergroup relationships. Fear of sexual aggression by the Negro was strong. Fear was abundant that Negroes and Okies might move into respectable neighborhoods, usurp the seats of street-cars, or spoil the exclusive tone of places of entertainment and friendly gathering. All these anxieties attacked the sense of security in social prestige and privilege, and the right of freer, fuller living in the world, which accrued to the elite by virtue of prior possession and superior qualifications.

The defenses of the ego clung with the dependency of ivy to these sturdy shafts of privilege, and the emotional agitations of threatened loss were as tumultuous as ivy in a wind. Emotionalism, indeed, was almost the whole of the shipyard attitude toward minorities. The response to any encroachment upon privilege was thus immediate, automatic, and stereotyped. Axioms of speech and action were always readily available to express the resistance of the elite to the claims of a minority. The heavy weight of "Woman's place is in the home" fell upon the shipyard women. Other minorities were surrounded by similar timeworn judgments. The Negro group in particular was the target of a barrage of rigid formulas of rejection. The commentary of the maleficent elite regarding this rebellious group was like the cant of a witch doctor bent upon conquering a demon let loose. Over and over again the same concepts, the same phrases, recurred.

Shipyard emotionalism further tended to magnify small adjustments and realignments of the status quo into wholesale catastrophes. To give an inch, it was assumed by the misers of prestige, was ultimately to lose the world. This reaction most readily occurred in the area of Negro-white relationships, where sexual intercourse between one Negro man and one white woman immediately assumed the proportions of the ravishing of a race, or where the advance of a few Negro families into a white neighborhood was feared as much as if it were the premonitory spray of a tidal wave of color.

Shipyard antagonisms against the presumption of minorities had entangled roots which reached down to the primitive bedrock of the individual psyche, down to the inmost source of human hate and love and fear and confidence. To understand them fully would require a long excursion through the labyrinth of man, his nature and his history. But in the narrower circuit of the shipyard world it was sufficiently apparent how important and precious a possession of any member of the elite was the consciousness of his innate and rightful superiority to all lesser peoples. His affection for this birthright was to be matched in intensity only by his horror at the possibility of its loss. Hence his eternal vigilance against the dangers which he imagined to threaten it from every side; and hence his hatred against the minorities whose least stirrings he interpreted as attacks upon the citadel of his security.

The economic rivalry afforded by minority groups was an additional occasion for anxiety among the ship-

yard elite. This rivalry was open, obvious, and in terms
of substantive fact even more dangerous than claims
upon the area of social prestige. In an economy subject
to fits of colic in which were regurgitated multitudes of
workers who apparently had long since been digested,
the addition of any new group to the menu was not
welcomed by those already on it. The unions were the
official spokesmen for opposition to this intrusion, and
as long as they could withstand the pressures of war
they excluded from the skilled trades every shipyard
minority, and in doing so reflected the views of the membership. The skilled worker himself, however, seldom
used the economic argument, logical though it was,
against the minorities. He turned instead to emotional
protests against close contact and unfitness. He resisted
the intrusion of women because of its affront to propriety. As for the Negro, the economic argument was
overwhelmed in the mass of hates and fears which
blocked the race from the union and advancement on the
job, and likewise from social contact and opportunity.

The shipyard does not therefore bear out a rigid and
orthodox statement of certain theories about the primacy of economic rivalry in the genesis and maintenance of minority problems. Unquestionably the facts
of economic rivalry played an important part in the
motivation of intergroup antagonism in the shipyards,
but in prevalent expressions of this antagonism other

anxieties and other arguments were found to dominate. Economic rivalry between racial or pseudoracial groups was only one aspect of a larger competitiveness which included also a struggle for various types of social privilege. In this maze of conflict it is as impossible to separate a cause from its consequences as it is to find the beginning of a wheel.

It has been made apparent, furthermore, with particular clarity where the Negro is concerned, that the citadel of inequality is most readily attacked and penetrated through the portal of economic restrictions and discriminations. The fact is indicated by the extreme rarity—almost the nonexistence—of white workers in the shipyards who expressed themselves as willing to admit the Negro to social equality with themselves in comparison with the substantially greater number who avowed acceptance of the Negro's right to a larger measure of economic opportunity. The shipyards themselves, and the presence within them of numbers of differing groups who worked in harmony and on a level of formal equality, provided even more impressive proof of the relative ease with which this breach in the wall of prejudice could be accomplished. It is difficult to understand or logically to explain the choice of values exhibited in these facts, for in terms of life and its necessities the monopoly of an area of employment would certainly appear to be more vital and more worthy of an obstinate defense than the monopoly of a neighborhood or a dance hall. But such was not the actual judgment, for men who would have butchered in frenzy and willingly have spent the last breath of their lives, if the sanctity of their homes had been threatened by the trespassing of a minority group, contented themselves with malevolent mutterings and promises of eventual revenge at sight of the invasion of their jobs. These men were, of course, by no means as much masters of the conditions of their employment as masters of their homes; theirs was not the will which initially determined what workers were to participate in the industrial activities of the nation, nor, indeed, was it the will of any person or any group which was ultimately responsible, so much as it was the unavoidable requirements of a cold materialism. The needs of an ever-expanding economy had for decades effectively submerged or nullified the cries of protest against increasing liberalization of job monopolies and, in combination with the restlessness of the deprived minorities, had broken barrier after barrier of prejudice and opened the fields of economic opportunity to the very groups which the shipyards eventually contained. Thus, whatever the explanation, this fact was reaffirmed in the shipyard: that adjustments in the traditional inequalities between groups were most readily made through economic relationships. In this sense, anxiety about

economic rivalry was indeed the most fundamental of
the fears which troubled the sleep of the shipyard elite,
since the destruction of the economic bulwarks provided
the most expedient path for further change.

In the technical conception of the term and its most
common usage, a minority group is no more than a
minor element in the population of an area, a small collection of people whose disabilities are intimately related to their insignificant numbers. At first glance, the
minorities of America appear to conform to this conception, since the largest American minority group,
the Negro, is only ten per cent of the total population
of the country. But when more minute inquiry is made
into the problem of minorities and the restrictions under
which they live, it is seen that the factor of inferior size
alone is not a sufficient explanation of their inferior
status. Over the broad face of America the liberties of
the Negro, for example, tend to vary not directly but
inversely with his numbers, and the battlements of prejudice stand tallest in the South, in some areas of which
he is in the majority. Likewise, prejudice against Ori-
entals and Mexicans is strongest, respectively, in California and the Southwest, where the largest numbers of
them reside or have resided. Indeed, when the fact is
considered that all American minority groups taken together—all groups, that is, whose sphere of life is limited
by the prejudice of an Anglo-Saxon or Teutonic elite

which holds itself to be natively or racially superior—form almost a majority of the American population the inadequacy of the concept which points to the inferior size of a group as the entire or primary explanation of its minority disabilities is even more apparent.

In the shipyard, the three largest minorities, women, Negroes, and Okies, added up to an obvious numerical majority, and there remained a considerably smaller assemblage of the elite who ruled by virtue of their position and their long-established prestige rather than by virtue of their superior numbers. Hence the relationships which have been under scrutiny here were not relationships between minority groups and a numerical majority whose right to make decisions and determine policy was the privilege classically acceded to such groups by the rules of parliamentary procedure, but between a dominant elite and a host of lesser peoples which, though collectively a majority, had each been able to achieve only a minor share of power.

In explanation of this system of relationships the fact is unquestionably important that the various minorities tended to identify themselves, so far as circumstances permitted, with the attitudes and antagonisms of the elite. Herein, indeed, lay the secret of the power of the elite, for when any one minority was under fire from the big guns of established privilege, other minorities, out of gun range for the moment, would merrily con-

tribute their birdshot to the fray. The Negro, for example, was most bitterly hated by the Okies and was
feared and scorned by the white women. I remember
the excited whispering of two dark-skinned Portuguese
girls (whose minority status was twofold) when they
entered a streetcar on their way home from work and
found most of the seats occupied by Negro workers.
"Look at those niggers hogging all the seats," one girl
remarked to the other. "Niggers always get the seats
and the white people have to stand." In reply her companion muttered, "I can't stand niggers. I can't stand
their looks, I can't stand their smell, I can't stand anything about them." The Negroes, meanwhile, were prone
to despise the "white trash" from Oklahoma and other
states of the backward South and Southwest and to hate
the Jews with an intensity peculiar to their own group
and its suppressed resentment of persecution. Women
were disapproved by the men of all races and strata who
worked beside them. Each minority in its turn stood
alone; never did I find any recognition of the desirability of a coalition.

Groups of newcomers have commonly been classed
as minorities. The huddle of immigrants who came to
America after the nation had been founded and organized on the basis of Anglo-Saxon stock and traditions,
was assumed to form the prototype of the minority.
Their lowly status was attributed in part to their com-

ing late to a table where the best victuals had already been devoured. But the mere lateness of arrival would hardly explain their deprivations. The current elite were themselves latecomers, as compared with the Indians, but they managed to find some very tempting morsels. Well-armed latecomers have done well throughout history.

The minorities of the shipyards, however, were indeed latecomers to this particular realm of opportunity, and the recency of their arrival was an important factor in the difficulties they faced. The unprecedented intrusion of women, Negroes, and Okies into this sanctum of the craftsman was itself an argument to employ against their coming, or against their remaining when once the barriers to entrance had been broken down. The dignity and strength which custom inherently possessed as custom was made to serve effectively against the uncertain, timid champions of change. The most superficial examination of the statements of resistance to the claims of the shipyard minorities reveals many repetitions and variations on the theme of the intrinsic disreputability of innovation.

The source of the minority problem as it exists in the broad world of America and as it existed likewise in the narrow world of the wartime shipyards does not appear to have been found, however, either in the relatively insignificant size of the minority groups or in their relatively recent entrance into an area of established ownership. True, the smallness of a single minority, in relation to the combined forces of the elite and all other minorities which endeavor to link themselves with the elite and its attitudes, contributes to the weakness of that minority's resistance to discrimination; but smallness is not the source of the discrimination itself. That the typical American minority group is a recent invader of any area of economic or social opportunity retards its escape from the restrictions of its position; but newness does not produce or maintain the restrictions themselves. These factors are, then, no more than contributory to the minority status and its disabilities. They are not the central root from which it grows, nor yet the soil wherein it finds its life.

The attitudes of the shipyard elite toward the minorities with whom they worked had two interacting, yet separate, aspects. There was, first, the conviction that the minorities were inferior in mind and body and spirit, and thus rightly inferior in economic level and social station. Second, there was the fear that the inferiors might encroach upon the privileges of the elite; and whereas a comfortable contempt alone could spring from the mere assumption of the inadequacies of the minority groups, vehement hatred was the inevitable product of their presumptuousness. This fear of aggression, in turn, was twofold, for it included both a fear of the seizure by minorities of exclusive social privileges and the fear of their intrusion into areas of economic monopoly. These several prejudices and anxieties were the motive force behind the entire policy of discrimination, and though the elite was primarily responsible for publicizing them, the minorities helped keep them alive. For, rather than question the validity of the prejudices, each minority group sought to except itself from them and to shift the load to weaker and lesser peoples.

Only the final gathering together of the particular phenomena of shipyard antagonisms and attitudes is needed, to achieve the concept which explains and systematizes the whole: the vision of society as hierarchically constituted and dominated by the drives of competition. Within this context the problem of minorities, as its exists in the shipyard and in the world at large, finds its ultimate rationale; for in a society of class and caste it becomes impossible for differing groups, whatever the factors which distinguish them, to be arranged horizontally as the varieties of a species of plant would be ordered by a botanist. The rigidity of the hierarchical system of thought requires rather a vertical scale of weaker and stronger, poorer and richer, inferior and superior, and along this scale all groups must find a place, with one group only, at any specific time, occupying the commanding eminence of the elite.

Minorities, it is then obvious, are no more nor less than all those hosts of people whose position upon the scale of social and economic privilege is inferior to that of the elite. They are not so much groups of minor size as groups which have a minor share in the privileges of a given society, and they are best defined by the number of their disabilities. In the shipyards the minorities were the groups that were not composed of male workers of Anglo-Saxon or Teutonic stock, city-bred and industrially experienced. Under the floodlamp of this concept every nuance of shipyard attitude emerges in a new and sharper focus. The philosophy of the hierarchical society, which was the philosophy of status, dominated all shipyard thinking concerning the characteristics and relationships of differing groups. It has frequently been observed how precious a possession of the individual shipyard worker was the sense of status which accrued from affiliation with the group of the elite, while members of the various minorities likewise cherished whatever superiority they could command over lowlier peoples.

So far as status within the shipyard hierarchy implied superiority to other groups and involved external advantages—proper rewards for superior virtue and ability—of privilege and wider opportunity, that status was prized and guarded from disturbance and the whole hierarchical system was protected and sustained. Distrust of change was thus the inevitable corollary of the hierarchical society and the desire of the beneficiaries to maintain its tenuous stability; for change in itself becomes an evil, and the intruding stranger, the instrument of change, becomes automatically suspect in the view of a group which, through the least disruption of the delicate balance of its power, may lose part or all of its preëminence. The emphasis in shipyard belief upon race and sex and the whole area of biological or pseudobiological differences similarly achieves its full significance in conjunction with this concern for the preservation of an existent hierarchical society. The dogmatic assertion that native or racially determined inferiority always characterized a group of inferior status provided both justification for that status and the guarantee of its continuance, and conferred upon the arbitrary distinctions of social rank the dignity and permanence of the natural absolute.

But however deep the foundations of the structure of status were laid, however tall the fortress walls were raised, there was still the ever-present danger of rebellion; for insecurity and tension were inherent in the very concept which transformed horizontal differences between peoples, differences of language or accent, of skin color, and of cultural experience, into vertical distinctions in power and opportunity, and so far as the shipyard community was a tapestry of class and caste

they were likewise wrought into the elementary fila-
ments of its fabric. Since no position on the vertical
scale of shipyard privilege save that of the elite was
voluntarily chosen or cheerfully retained, a continuing
conflict among the minorities, discontented and disunited as they were, naturally ensued in the effort of
each to protect the station which it had and to rise yet
higher in the series. The group of the elite, however,
exalted though it was and circled with a thousand watch-
dogs of its sovereignty, appears at the last as unhappy
a constituent as any of the others in the class structure of shipyard society. Although possessing power, it
was both insecure in the continuance of that possession
and, in a world of infinite possibilities of ownership,
dissatisfied with the amount; for the members of this
topmost shipyard group conceived their privilege to be
threatened from two sides: from beneath by the host of
the less powerful and less well-situated minorities, who
struggled to seize what they, the elite, possessed, and
from above by the Jew, who endeavored to keep from
them the quintessence of empire which they coveted.

UNIONS

✿ THE STORY of the shipyards is
only half told when the influences contributing to disunity have been considered; there still remains the task
of observing and appraising the forces which inclined
toward unity and the degree of their success or the reasons for their failure. Since disunity was the inevitable
concomitant of emphasis upon race and racial differences, the appeal to unity had necessarily to supersede
this pattern of shipyard thinking and to find, for social
organization, a broader basis than kinship. The principles upon which shipyard disunities were established
and maintained stressed the natural, the absolute, and
the eternal; the principles which supported the claims
of unity, on the other hand, were overtly man-made and
institutional and were limited in their inclusiveness only
by particular conditions and passing circumstance. The
conflict between these two sets of principles and the two
differing points of view which they implied—as that
conflict involved the shipyard community and its heterogeneous inhabitants—constitutes the very core and substance of this analysis.

Numerous agencies of social unity played out their
roles of varying significance within the society of the
wartime shipyards. The labor unions were among the
most important of these agencies. The social outlook of

the typical shipyard union was not, even in theory, extraordinarily broad, nor did it represent a negation of the canons of intergroup competitiveness. Indeed, it was the traditional endeavor of every trade organization to establish as large as possible a domain of job monopoly and so to limit membership as to guarantee a scarcity value for the skill it represented. This protectionist spirit was exemplified in the resistance by the unions to the admission of shipyard minorities to full and equal membership. With very few exceptions or qualifications the account of the actual practices of the trade unions in the shipyard is a tale of narrowness and prejudice, similar to that which might be told of any established and privileged elite and its efforts to protect its vested interests from the claims of the disinherited mass.

The trade unions embodied, nonetheless, within the very elements of their structure a challenge to the biological or racial distinctions and disunities of the shipyards; for the purposes of these organizations involved no consideration of kinship principles, but rather turned to the common sharing of an economic interest as the sole basis of association. Not brotherhood in blood but brotherhood in the trade was the firm rock on which the union's solidarity was founded, and much of the ritual of the trade union and its gatherings was concerned with the transference of traditional loyalties from the confraternity of kinship to the confraternity of skill. Thus, when the throngs of newcomers were at last let in, they were absorbed—officially at least—into a unity which ignored all previous distinctions of caste, sex, or race.

The mere lowering of barriers to membership was not enough to make every worker an active collaborator in the unity of trade-union interests. Since the ship-building industry of the Bay Area was dominated by closed-shop agreements, all workers in the trades at Moore Dry Dock were nominally members of some trade union. This membership was highly qualified and limited, however, not only by the reluctance of the trade unions to encourage real participation by the newcom-ers, but also by the antagonism, indifference, and igno-rance of the newcomers themselves. For most of the shipyard workers—almost all the women, most of the Negroes and Okies, and many of the elite—the first job in the shipyards was also the first experience with a union. How few of them held union cards before com-ing to the yards was shown in a survey of the marine steamfitting and pipefitting trade. The Bay Area local of its union, an affiliate of the United Association of Journeymen Plumbers and Steamfitters of the United States and Canada, had a prewar membership of be-tween 350 and 400. In the summer of 1943 the mem-bership exceeded 17,000. Of these, a business agent of the union estimated, no more than 500 had transferred from other locals. Since men who held active member-

ship in unions in control of other trades naturally
tended to seek the shipyard craft in which they were
skilled, few marine steamfitters could be expected from
that source. Some oil workers from the California,
Texas, and Oklahoma fields, which had been partly
organized by the C.I.O., did find their way into the
trade, on the basis of similar previous work, but the
only other newcomers with some degree of union experience were the scattering of clerks and waitresses,
who, if they had worked in the Bay Area, or in any
other highly unionized region, were members of the
unions controlling their jobs. These several groups
totaled, in the opinion of the business agent, no more
than 2,000—not even one-seventh of the peak enroll-
ment. Similar statistics have undoubtedly obtained in
the other greatly expanded unions of the wartime shipyards. In the Marine Laborers' Union, which grew, after
Pearl Harbor, from 7 members to more than 30,000
drawn for the most part from the drifters and the unskilled, earlier union affiliation was rarer still.

Most workers entered the yards not merely ignorant
of unions, but distrustful of them. Much of what they
knew and felt about them had been acquired from newspaper accounts that were prejudiced, from the talk of
small businessmen and farmers who were antagonistic,
or from those occasional workers who, in having been
excluded from a trade by monopolistic union practices,

had even more impressive reasons for complaint. Fed by such reports as these, many came to think the union a menace rather than an aid to workers; at best it was alien to their interests and traditional loyalties.

To workers who had no union background and no knowledge of the principles of labor organization there was little or no appeal in the type of unity which the trade unions of the shipyard represented. They nonetheless joined the unions, as they were compelled to do, with little protest. They paid the initiation fees, averaging not more than twenty dollars, much as they would have bought a ticket to the county fair: it cost money, but maybe the show would be worth the outlay. As for dues, they paid them with resignation to the principle that all the joys of life are balanced by a measure of pain.

The amount of antagonism and larger amount of indifference to unions astonished me. The masses for whom the unions were presumably established possessed and nourished much of the same suspicion of unions and their purposes and much of the same bitterness against the levying of union fees as would be appropriate to a caucus of manufacturers. Although the thousands of shipyard workers were enjoying wages and working conditions which manifestly were the product of years of union struggle, they saw no connection between the dues they paid and the benefits they received.

On the contrary, it was commonly assumed that unions, like other businesses, existed for the benefit of the owners and managers—the horde of union officials who waxed fat on the take of their racket. "Unions are just rackets like horse racing or any other game that's set up to make money for the fellows in the know," one worker said. "They're not really on the side of the workingman, and they don't give any service for the money he puts in." When I asked him if he knew of some other organization with genuine concern for the worker, he named a large and paternal business firm; its recreation projects and health-insurance schemes were, he assured me, far superior to anything the unions had to offer.

Since I was a shop steward of my own union and stood in the relation of publicist to it and its policies, I had personal experience of resistance to unions and to their claims on the membership. At the time of the State election campaign of 1944, for example, a proposed amendment to the California constitution would in effect have declared the closed shop illegal. Almost all the union locals of the Bay Area, after obtaining the approval of their members in open meeting, levied an assessment of one dollar on each member to finance a fight against the amendment. Grumbling over this assessment was widespread, and I was frequently challenged to defend its validity and even informed by skeptical members of my own union of their intention not to pay. The bulkheads of the ships and the walls of storerooms and tool shacks were often chalked with such expressions as "The union is hungry again. Dig deep, boys, and give her another dollar."

No matter what action a union took or what policy it pursued, there were always those who discovered underhand designs. The Steamfitter's Union, for instance, as one of its several projects for more fully interesting its membership, opened a series of training classes in which members could obtain free instruction in various branches of their trade. No worker to whom I explained this opportunity received the information with gratitude or enthusiasm, but many were skeptical of its value and its actual intent. "That school is just somebody's scheme to make a wad of easy dough," one worker said. "You can't fool me that a bunch of union officers are going to go out of their way to help the workingman."

Union officers and business agents were reputed to receive enormous salaries and to supplement their legitimate earnings with large sums either stolen outright or taken as bribes for favors. "These business agents are a gang of robbers," a shipyard worker grumbled. "They drive around in Cadillacs and live like millionaires while us ordinary working guys pay through the nose." Purity of intention was scarcely admitted as a possibility among those who sought or obtained an official position in a union. On the occasion of an annual election of the Steamfitter's Union, the skeptics of the yards had a specially merry time impugning the motives of those office seekers with whom they worked and were closely acquainted. They said of one candidate for business agent that he was in danger of losing his shipyard job because he lacked competence to keep it, and so was frantically in search of a soft and profitable berth elsewhere; and of another office seeker, that he had a girl friend whom he was anxious to impress with something more than a shipyard salary. A worker who "on principle" refused to take part in this election explained that he could see no reason for troubling himself to push one bunch of pigs away from the trough merely to make room for another.

So thoroughly convinced were most shipyard workers of the corruption of union officialdom that, although they protested frequently enough, they appeared almost to take these activities for granted as part of an inevitably exploitive world and to consider anyone a fool who did not profit from them when he had a chance. As a shop steward, for example, I was believed to be within reaching distance of the union swag, and was advised again and again by my well-wishers in the shipyards to make the most of my opportunities for personal enrichment. "That union has plenty of money," I was told; "if you don't get it, somebody else sure will." My reiterations of enthusiasm for the cause of union labor and hence of indifference to such proposals at first were not believed, and later were viewed as evidence of abnormality. Idealism, whether real or specious, was not considered by the average shipyard worker to be worthy of regard or emulation.

Unions were also resented as dictatorial powers which on occasion demanded inconvenient and even odious obedience. In the fall of 1944 the Moore Dry Dock Company, in order to complete a contract on schedule—or so the reason was stated,—requested that the day-shift workers in several crafts, including steamfitting, start work at six o'clock in the morning instead of seven. Most of the workers objected to this advance in starting time, although the extra hour would have brought overtime pay; after some dispute the Steamfitters' Union followed the lead of the Machinists' and issued a blanket command forbidding its members, on pain of a fine, to start work until seven o'clock. This order was generally popular, but on publicizing it I found dissenters. "I hope you and your two-bit union never get another nickel's worth of overtime," one worker flung at me, and many others complained with almost equal vigor. "It was easy for me to come in at six o'clock, and I needed the extra money, too," a woman worker said. "I don't see what right the union has to keep me from doing what I want to do." The average worker's conception of the union as an organization distant from him and his interests was expressed not only in such resentment against it and its compulsions, but also in a certain timidity before the irresponsible power which he believed it to embody. One of the business agents of my union complained, for example, that the members he met in the yards tended to approach him hat in hand, much as if they were in the presence of a front-office manager. "They think I'm there just to check their dues books," he said despondently, "and that I'll fire them on the spot if they haven't kept their payments up to date."

Occasionally, though not as often as intense propaganda from certain antiunion factions would appear to warrant, I came upon the charge in shipyard talk that a particular union policy subverted the broader needs of the nation and the war. At the time of a three-day walkout by the Machinists' Union, the only C.I.O. affiliate at Moore Dry Dock, some workers in the crafts adversely affected by the creeping paralysis were so much incensed as to ask for governmental intervention and severe discipline of the union. One man antagonistic to the C.I.O. proclaimed that the strikers were all "a bunch of radicals" and that the Navy should take over and crush the recalcitrants. "What they ought to do with those strikers," another advised, "is to put a rifle on their shoulders and, without bothering with any training, ship them right across to fight the Japs." A few workers in the yards went so far as to consider all union enterprise as subversive. One steamfitter, in search of lunchtime reading matter, refused my offer of a copy of the newspaper of his union with the remark, "I don't want to read no communist sheet." Another worker said that, so far as he was concerned, "all unions were communist" and ought to be avoided by the decent, law-abiding, Christian citizen. But these were extreme responses from extremely antagonistic persons who stood on the outer fringes of the confused suspicion of unions which characterized the common viewpoint.

The split between the A. F. of L. and the C.I.O. appreciably shaped the union attitudes of the workers at Moore Dry Dock. The mere existence of the split increased the antagonism to the unions. As a member and shop steward of an A. F. of L. union, I became keenly conscious of the bitterness nurtured toward the upstart C.I.O. In union meetings and shipyard discussions equally, the dispute was feudlike. To one steamfitter, who had grown gray in the trade and union, the C.I.O. was a raider on the domain of respectable trade unionism; as a result of its activities the heyday of American trade unions, which he placed in the 'twenties, had passed beyond all hope of return. "The C.I.O., with its communist bastards and its nigger flunkies," he said, "has wrecked trade unionism in this country for good and for all." His extreme partisanship was not widely shared; few workers were interested enough, or well enough informed about the issues in the quarrel, to take sides so positively. A more representative response was that of a man who before his present affiliation with an A. F. of L. union had been in the C.I.O. United Automobile Workers. "When I was a member of the C.I.O.," he remarked, "I was for the C.I.O., and now that I'm a member of the A.F.L., I'm for the A.F.L. I'm for whatever bunch I happen to belong to." Skepticism joined opportunism in dividing American labor. "How can you expect people to get together with the unions," a worker asked, "if the unions can't even get together with themselves?"

Lethargic disinterest in union activities and problems was well-nigh universal. The seventeen thousand members of the steamfitters' and pipefitters' local were usually represented at the bimonthly meetings by fewer than a hundred workers, most of whom were a tightly knit group of prewar members who assiduously attended in the hope of protecting their established power. The local's two annual elections held in the course of my two-year affiliation were of basic importance to the organization, but no more than one-eighth of the membership voted. I was particularly active in one of the campaigns, and know that it was widely publicized. I distributed hundreds of bulletins and pamphlets de-

scribing the persons and problems in the dispute, but
for the most part the members showed no interest in the
information and often caustically rejected it. I was also
the agent for soliciting free subscriptions to the newspaper representing the organization and all the unions
of the Bay Area Metal Trades Council. The member
had only to fill out a postcard which was already
stamped and addressed, but four out of five of those
whom I approached refused the offer. "Why, all a newspaper's good for, anyway, is to line a garbage can,"
said one of them, "and the Sunday funnies take care of
that around our house." Moore Dry Dock was not exceptional in its resistance to this offer, moreover, for
out of the total membership of the Steamfitters' Union
only some two thousand workers requested delivery of
the paper.

Reluctance to participate in union functions was
prevalent among the workers in all the shipyard trades.
Their apathy to the claims upon their loyalty appeared
to yield to persuasion, but actually did not allow a single
shaft of enthusiasm to penetrate. I have watched union
organizers of the old line, grizzled in the service, fling
themselves against this apathy with all the futile force
of exasperation. I have heard them waste more vitupera-
tion upon their own uncoöperative members than they
ever directed at the machinations of capital. One of the
business agents of my own union, in a moment of aban-

don, poured forth to me a torrent of complaint about the workers to whom he felt that he had dedicated his life. "I sometimes think," he said, "that the working stiff is the most ungrateful man on earth. The union slaves for him and fights for him, and there's them as are in it who are ready to go to jail for him, and then he begrudges the little dues he pays, won't even come to the meetings, and spreads slander around that a few of us guys are getting rich out of the union till." Another worker at Moore Dry Dock, an organizer in former days, was similarly incensed by the apathy of the shipyard union members. "All they ever think about is not what they can give to a union, but what they can get out of it. If you reduced their dues to fifty cents a month, gave them ten dollars a week in sick benefit, cut them in on a five-hundred-dollar life-insurance policy, and kept free beer on ice at the union hall besides, then maybe a few of them would get off their fat cans and come to a union meeting now and then. If everybody would only work together," he added, "there's nothing within reason that we couldn't do or get. But the way things are, twenty per cent are trying to legislate for eighty per cent, and the eighty per cent don't give a damn."

The shipyard worker's attitude toward the union had, however, its positive as well as its negative phase. Apathetic and often suspicious though he was concerning unions and their activities, the worker was nonetheless also aware of his weakness as a propertyless individual before the oppressive power of wealth. David, the stranger to heavy industry, confronted the Goliath of capitalism, and stood there alone without his slingshot. How prevalent and deep-seated an enmity resulted from this sense of personal impotence was evident in the intensity of hatred of the Jew, who was capitalism personified. It required, therefore, only an open outburst of the latent conflict between worker and employer to convince the worker that—for the time being, at any rate—he should unite with his fellows in protection of their common interest. If a clear-cut dispute occurred between management and a group of employees, and the newspapers blazed with headlines condemning the workmen, the membership of the union under attack customarily rallied round its standards; with amazing rapidity a sprawling, disunited cluster became almost an integrated group. The union's discipline was then accepted with little complaint, even if it meant the loss of several days' pay because a strike was called. In my years at Moore Dry Dock two strikes were called, and were energetically supported. The Machinists' Union conducted the more important and long-lasting of the two strikes, and was, throughout, the stormy petrel of the yard. It appeared also to be the union which evoked the most consistent and spirited devotion of its members. The one occasion when the Steamfitters ran afoul of company rulings and challenged the change of starting time was likewise the occasion which brought the membership closely together. In winning the dispute, the union also temporarily won over its members.

Jurisdictional disputes between the unions tended to awaken in the rival memberships some of the same sense of unity, and individual representatives of the quarreling groups frequently took it upon themselves to advocate collective interests with their own fists. But the unity established in all these conflicts lasted no longer than the threat that caused them. After the excitement had died away, the old indifference and cynicism invariably returned. There is little evidence that permanent or widespread change in the typical worker's view of unions was accomplished as a result of his few years of shipyard experience. The wartime shipyard, it must be noted, like wartime industry as a whole, presented peculiar obstacles to the unions which made it impossible for them to conduct the type of proselytizing campaign among their members that had been the accustomed procedure of the past. Wartime controls on industrial and economic activities were so numerous and so powerful that individual unions were scarcely able to affect them, and much of the historical function of the unions was temporarily lost. They could do little more than preserve the status quo. Such battles as the

Bay Area unions conducted involved no big issues and, even if concluded to the workers' satisfaction, aroused no great enthusiasm. With rare and trivial exceptions, the great unifying force of the strike was absent. Of the two strikes that did occur, the longer lasted only three days, was conducted by one union alone, and was directly concerned with the grievance of a mere handful of its members. Most shipyard workers who lacked experience with unions and their service to the workingman thus had little opportunity to observe what unions could accomplish on a free field of combat. Even those few who had been through hard times with a union tended to forget previous benefits and to complain because more were not forthcoming now. Emasculated as the shipyard unions seemed, surrounded by the controls of a state at war as they were, it was little wonder that their fretting members frequently asked, "What good is a union to us? What service can it perform for us now?"

Other techniques than dramatic conflict between labor and capital were available to the unions for the demonstration of their usefulness to the wage earner. There were, for instance, the techniques of the schoolroom, with their emphasis on vicarious participation in significant occurrences through reading about them in books or hearing about them from an eyewitness. There were also the pamphlet, the lecture, and the persuasive argument. Such procedures have never been entirely neglected in American labor unions, but until the emergence of the C.I.O., with its more extensive political and economic vision, neither were they emphasized. Trade unions typically had moved from one overt conflict to another, and since the issues of each dispute were narrow, specific, and completely familiar to the membership, indirect methods of indoctrination were not required. But with the recent surge in union membership, with the attendant stabilization of relationships between capital and labor, and with the whole broadening of union activities and principles to fill a broader economic and political field—processes all well under way before the war—a need arose for different and more flexible techniques to establish, maintain, and extend the unity of labor. To this need the C.I.O. responded more readily and more fully than the A. F. of L. Indeed, the C.I.O. itself emerged in large part from the hopeful effort to discover new solutions to the new problems which the calcified traditions of the Federation could not solve.

The impulses of the war only increased the tempo of a change which had been long developing amid the conventionalities of the American labor movement. Shipyard unions which had been quietly settling in eddies and peaceful pools were caught by the freshet of the emergency and were swept, protesting, into the central

current of the times. With the exception of the C.I.O.
Machinists, the unions in control of the ship-construction
trades at Moore Dry Dock were affiliates of the A. F. of
L., had previously been small in numbers, and had been
sustained through many a hard-won battle by the *esprit
de corps* traditional in a company of skilled and closely
protected workmen. They had developed no procedure
for similarly unifying the swarms of men and women
who now flocked into their several societies. Having
never before made extensive use of the techniques of
education in dealing with their members, they were
neither equipped nor inclined to do so now.

The incoming worker was subjected to but one contact with the traditions of the shipyard unions—the brief
and often utterly inane ceremony of initiation. Thereafter the unions for the most part left their new members unmolested, except to insist that they regularly pay
their dues, a transaction which was usually conducted
through the sterile channels of the postal service. Except in the one bright hour of their initiation, most union
members never saw the headquarters of their union,
never met their union officers, and never read or heard
about the principles on which their union was established or the agreements by which it operated.

Exceptional unions with exceptionally progressive
policies did, of course, exist even in the American Federation of Labor. One or two of the unions at Moore

Dry Dock attempted an active campaign of education
to increase the participation of their members in union
affairs. The Steamfitters undertook the most noteworthy
of these endeavors, under the guidance of a forward-
looking group which, after long and bitter conflict with
entrenched conservatism, finally gained control. Classes
were opened to all who desired further instruction in
their trade, union newspapers were distributed free of
charge, and meeting places were arranged for the con-
venience of the scattered membership. The union also
instituted, as perhaps the most ambitious and effective
of its enterprises, a shop-steward system by means of
which the grievances of the workers were brought directly to the union officers and union policies were in
turn relayed to the members. Thus the few who had
begun to appreciate labor unity were stimulated to keep
the general membership reminded of its coherence.

In most other shipyard unions the pressure for the
institution of similar policies was never sufficient to
overcome the stolid resistance of the elders. The reluctance of the labor organizations to make more than the
traditional gestures of welcome to their wartime members was due in part to their inability to adjust to the
irregular circumstances of the period, and in part to
their unfamiliarity with the problems so suddenly presented; but it was also due to the cynicism which branded
the new workers as incompetent and temporary acces-

sions, who, once the war boom spent itself, must lose their jobs and return to fields and sinks. Why teach such masses about the spirit of unionism if the effort was doomed to failure?

The cost of the usual educational methods was a further argument against them; they would exhaust the slowly gathered funds which were the union's assurance of power in the event of future conflict with capital. This objection to the extravagance of educational methods was formidable and, even in my own more liberal union, a frequently incontestable complaint. To print and mail a single bulletin of union news, or a notice of a meeting, to the seventeen thousand members of the Bay Area local of the Steamfitters' Union cost six or seven hundred dollars, and the returns, if any were discernible, were hard to measure.

The principal basis, however, for the hesitancy of the trade unions of the old line to initiate a widespread and energetic educational campaign among their members was the hostility which their leaders retained toward real union participation by the newcomers. Never having welcomed them, the unions now preferred not to stimulate their loyalty and enthusiasm, but to place and keep them at a secondary level of membership and to protect for future exploitation by the few the inner citadel of the union and the vested interest which it represented. The Boilermakers' Union of the San Fran-

cisco area arranged to freeze its officers in their positions
for the duration and finally went so far as to suspend
all meetings of the membership for a period of two
years. A similar but unsuccessful effort was made by
certain of the leaders of the Steamfitters, and no doubt
by other fearful politicians in other shipyard unions.
Where such drastic methods did not succeed, a campaign of petty tyranny and discrimination against the
newcomers—against "Okies," "niggers," and women—
was persistently continued. Thus the very persons within
the unions who most scornfully derided the shipyard
worker's ignorance and indifference were also those who
cherished and promoted these attitudes most jealously
as the foundation of their own tenure of power.

These protectionistic and monopolistic policies were
decried by union leaders whose outlook was broader
and who knew the value of enlightening even the most
temporary members, in the hope that, wherever they
might go, they would spread abroad an atmosphere favorable to the spirit of organization. But these few could
do little more than inveigh against the absence of a for-
ward-looking educational policy. One among them, a
business agent of the Steamfitters, on looking back from
the spring of 1945 when the shipyard population was
already well along in the process of decline, declared
his bitter disappointment with the lack of positive accomplishment by the unions in the war years. He felt

that of the workers who had come to the wartime ship-yard from farms and shop counters at the beginning of the war, few were returning with different or more en-lightened attitudes. After a year, or two or three years, of nominal union membership they were leaving to re-form the same old residue of prejudice against the principles of organization which, even more than the antagonism of capital, was the source of labor's previ-ous difficulties. "The unions missed the bus," he said; "they completely missed the bus, and all you can hope for now is that, if the same chance ever comes again, they'll know enough to do a better job of it."

CLASS CONSCIOUSNESS

✿ MANY ECONOMISTS have pointed out that workingmen in a capitalistic society have in common many problems and interests which are at the same time peculiar to them in their function as wage earners in a system primarily aimed at profit making. A similarity of status and economic role, it has frequently been asserted, envelops this great majority of contemporary society in a single category or class as real and determinate as any other human grouping, and sets it off, moreover, from other, smaller class divisions whose concerns are different and competitive. To the workingmen's full awareness of this unity of interest which binds them all—or to class consciousness, as it has been termed—certain theorists and reformers have assigned a tremendously dynamic and creative role in the processes of social change, and have seen it as a first and necessary step toward the achievement of the ultimate equalitarian ideal, the end of classes and the destruction of all status.

In contemporary America, distinctions of economic class are not so plainly marked by peculiarities of dress and traditional restrictions on activity as they have been in the historic past and as they still are in certain areas of Europe. Yet the slightest searching of the facts of social living will reveal that even in America economic classes do exist and that the class interests of the poor man and the rich man, the worker and the employer, are distinct if not conflicting. Class consciousness, however, as the theorists have conceived it, implies not only the factual unity of labor's interest, but also complete awareness of that unity by labor. Here the ground for investigation becomes less firm. Class consciousness *per se* is not commemorated or solidified in America by any obvious and definite symbol or formal institution. Trade unions which, theoretically viewed, are capable of incorporating the vast masses of the wage earners and testifying to their existence as a distinct and compact class are themselves too much torn with dissension and the disintegrating practices of competition to represent the unity of labor in more than an extremely tentative and partial manner. It is, then, only as a complex of attitudes that class consciousness can have an existence, and being no more than this, it might seem too imponderable for investigation. But it does embody an appeal to social unity which is a long step beyond that offered by the labor unions, and it proclaims the need of disregarding differences of sex, race, and culture in favor of larger continuities of economic status and class interest. Therefore, despite the difficulties of the search, an effort to discover among the workers of the shipyards some evidence of their consciousness of common interests as an economic class is worth while.

Workers in the yards were well aware of the hierarchical arrangement of society and of the differences in social status, in wealth and privilege, which characterize different groups of men in the modern world. Their own shipyard community was, in their view, a sort of ladder, with an elite at the universally coveted top and a descending series of minority groupings discontentedly occupying the lower rungs. Yet they thought of this structure in terms not of economic differences or diversities of economic function, but of biological or racial distinctions, and interpreted the particular economic or social status of each group as a secondary consequence of biological equipment. In making these biological distinctions, moreover, they totally disregarded the common interests of all workingmen; and because emphasis was placed upon the narrow consciousness of racial caste, the distinctions drawn were antipathetic to the much more extended and inclusive consciousness of economic class. The emergence of class consciousness among the workers of the shipyards was obstructed rather than aided by the concept of the structure and constituents of the social hierarchy which they entertained.

With respect to one racial group, however, a measure of correspondence existed between the concepts of the racial hierarchy and the concepts of class distinction developed by the economic theorist. The Jew, as the

shipyard worker comprehended him, was the capitalistic class personified. In him was embodied resentful
recognition by the various competing groups of the shipyard hierarchy of the fact that they were all surrounded,
the elite and the deprived minorities alike, by a world
of power and privilege to which no ordinary workingman could lay claim. In their belief that they shared a
common injustice as victims of Jewish greed, the shipyard groups were at least united in hatred of the presumed agent of their insufficiencies. To be united in
hatred of an external enemy, however, is not necessarily
to be united in mutual and internal trust, and even this
faint touch of class consciousness was a negative rather
than a positive imprint.

The complex of attitudes which constitutes class consciousness does not envisage the unity of all society,
as society exists in the modern, civilized, and capitalistic world, but only the unity of a single class within
that society, the class of wage earners, which it sharply
demarcates from other classes. It has therefore a twofold aspect and encompasses both a negative and a positive argument. The positive argument is the plea for
unity among all workingmen, the plea on which the
revolutionary proclamation, "Workers of the world,
unite!" is founded. The negative argument, from which,
according to the theorists, the positive must inevitably
eventuate, is the attack upon the class or classes in capi-

talistic society which do not work for wages, but, instead, live either directly on indirectly on the profits extorted from the labor of the producing mass. Only the negative argument was prominent in the shipyards, and, even so, was confused and seldom emerged in fully developed form. The shipyard workers were undoubtedly opposed to many aspects of the world of capitalism which restricted their area of freedom and limited their opportunities for personal achievement and aggrandizement.

They were, for instance, unanimous in their disapproval of excessive wealth, or at least of the possessors of such wealth, and they concentrated and solidified this disapproval in hatred of the Jew. The wealthy person, even if not a Jew, and the man of authority, social prestige, and conspicuous accomplishments, were inherently suspect in the shipyard view, which, for reasons hardly theological, had achieved the Christian presumption that the rich merchant was hardly to be numbered among the blessed.

This fact was well illustrated by shipyard reactions to a sensational murder trial which was held, in the summer of 1944, in a small town near by, and in which the defendant, a woman of means and social position, was accused of killing in jealousy the young son of an obscure and poverty-stricken farmer. The shipyard audience avidly devoured the newspapers' garish details of the daily sessions of the court. They were not, however, sifting evidence with an eye to justice; they prejudged the case from their first knowledge of its broad outlines. To them the dead farm boy was, in an obscure way, a martyred representative of their own kind; so the woman was judged guilty before she stepped upon the stand. Her eventual acquittal was merely cited as further evidence of the iniquity and influence of wealth.

The realm of luxury was far from the average shipyard worker and was therefore subject to the elaborations of the myth. Free as a dream from logical constraints, the myth made room for innumerable confusions and contradictions. On one side was the concept of the wickedness which characterized the gold-possessing few; tales were told and accepted of women of wealth who wantonly murdered their hapless paramours, of bankers who plotted the ravishment of the nation and the heartless exploitation of the poor. On the other side was the concept of the fantastic fairyland of pleasure to which such wickedness provided entrance. The physical surroundings of wealth, well known through the stylized presentations of the motion picture, were embellished by imagination and were unashamedly dwelt upon as objects of desire. I remember one shipyard worker's ecstatic report of his prewar visit as a plumber to one of the mansions of the San

Francisco peninsula. "It was a palace fit for a king!" he exclaimed. "The rugs were soft as velvet; the staircase was of marble, and even the toilet seats had ermine cushions on 'em. Jeez, when I saw that joint, I just wanted to move in and stay forever."

This intermixture of righteous disapproval of excessive wealth or exalted status and envy of the joy of its possession was characteristic of all shipyard reactions to the actualities of a hierarchical society. Just as the shipyard minorities who fretted under the restrictions of their position never attacked the system of discrimination itself, but rather sought to push some other group aside and climb a little higher, the shipyard worker who observed the fuller enjoyment of the world's good things by those who were more powerful and more fortunate did not condemn the conventionalities of privilege, but rather complained because another than himself had usurped the place he coveted. I once chanced to start a discussion concerning the distinctions between the quarters then being outfitted with chromium fixtures and luxurious bunks for a ship's officers and the much more utilitarian quarters for the crew. I questioned whether the degree of this distinction was necessary or desirable or just, but my doubt was not echoed. The general reaction was neatly put in one worker's remark: "Well, hell! It's a sweet setup if you happen to be a captain."

The same confused interplay of attitude and counter-
attitude was evident in relationships between workers
and their bosses. The many degrees of authority varied
from that possessed by the leaderman, who directed
the activities of a squad of eight or nine men and who
was paid a few more dollars weekly than they, to that
of the front-office big shot who was rarely in direct contact with the men of the yards and all the details of
whose daily round attested to the exaltation of his position. To every such variation in authority the worker
responded with a variation in attitude and behavior.
The use of first names, for instance, was ironclad custom among the ordinary workers. Whatever a shipyard
worker's age or personality, he was John or Bill or
Henry to his fellows and to all his supervisors. The
leaderman was usually included in this friendly circle, and so were many of the quartermen who desired
to maintain familiar relations with their larger gangs
of men. The significance of the manner of address was
indicated to me by a fellow worker who noticed that,
although I had been several weeks on the job, I still
greeted formally those with whom I was not well
acquainted. "When you call me by my last name," he
said, "it's like you were making fun of me somehow by
pretending I'm more important than I am." For it was
only the foreman and those of higher rank who were
invariably addressed by their last names, although if

their work remained within the area of construction their names were seldom preceded by the honorary title of "Mister." The men of the front office, however, who wore business suits and, carrying notebooks and brief-cases, occasionally wandered through the yards, were always spoken of as "Mr." Jones or "Mr." Brown, and the worker who had occasion to talk with them did so with an air of servility and due respect which might extend to the removal of his hat.

It was amusing to watch the sudden transformation whenever word got round that the foreman was on the hull or in the shop or that a front-office superintendent was coming by. Quartermen and leadermen would rush to their groups of workers and stir them to obvious activity. "Don't let him catch you sitting down," was the universal admonition, and where no work existed a semblance of work was devised for the moment. A piece of scrap pipe was busily bent and threaded, or a bolt which was already firmly in place was subjected to further and unnecessary tightening. This was the formal tribute invariably attending a visitation by the boss, and its conventions were as familiar to both sides as those surrounding a five-star general's inspection. To have neglected any detail of the false and empty show would have been interpreted as a mark of singu-lar disrespect. A quarterman I knew, who, out of an abounding good humor and an almost adolescent effervescence of personality, had never seriously tried to keep the customary barriers between himself and his men, once ruefully complained that his gang, skillful and diligent though they were, did not show proper deference to his position. "When I happen on the boys," he said, "and find them shooting craps because there's nothing else for them to do, they don't jump up like the gangs of other bosses do and hide the dice and act as if they'd been busy all the time. They just sit there and without so much as changing the expression of their faces ask me if maybe I won't join them in the game. I don't believe they've got an ounce of respect for me and my rating."

A job inevitably involved a hierarchy of authority. There was always a boss, and it was accepted shipyard dogma that it was the worker's place to do what the boss commanded and to do it without hesitation or question. "What a fellow learns on his first job, if he learns nothing else," I was told by an old-timer, "is to take the boss's orders and to keep his own mouth shut. I used to try and tell a boss if I knew he was wrong about a job, but after being tossed out on my ear a time or two I soon learned better. Now I do the thing just like the foreman tells me to, even if I'm sure it will get torn down and have to be put in different when the real big shots come snooping around. The way I figure it, that's the boss's worry and none of mine."

A large admixture of antagonism was part of this pattern of servility toward the boss; for the basis of the boss's dominance was not primarily the common recognition of his superiority in skill and knowledge, but the workers' fear of his ascendancy over them and their jobs. It was not so much the boss himself who was respected, as his power to hire and fire. I seldom heard a group of shipyard workers admit that a boss's superior skill and knowledge justified the position he held; I frequently heard them ridicule his pretensions and assert their own capacity to do better and judge more wisely. He was also subject to suspicion because of the talebearing, hypocrisy, and bootlicking by which they presumed he had achieved his position. The "company man" was the man who got ahead. A foreman of the plumbers was often a target for such charges. "That guy," a worker said, "he don't know nothing about plumbing; all he knows is how to lick the boots of the fellow higher up." The ruthless elimination of possible rivals was deemed to be a further tactic necessary to advancement, and the boss was therefore automatically branded as a person of doubtful morality and few scruples. One worker obliquely presented this opinion by explaining his own lack of success. "I never had the brass," he declared, "to kick another fellow in the teeth so I could get ahead myself. That's why, I guess, I ain't no farther up the ladder than I am."

The shipyard worker's antagonism to authority increased in direct ratio with his external servility, and
was most highly developed in the attitudes which he
reserved for the man of the front office. The rareness
of direct contact between them prevented any softening
of the traditional distinctions or any mollifying of the
underdog's resentment. The worker may have dropped
his eyes or removed his hat in the presence of front-
office men, but he thumbed his nose as soon as their
backs were turned. Their eminence was accepted as
beyond the reach of the ordinary worker. A driving
ambition might raise him to foreman, but never, save
through the most extraordinary turn of fortune's
wheel, to company manager. Managerial positions were
thought to be exclusively the gifts of preëxistent wealth
and privilege, and as a consequence the shipyard
worker's distrust of the front-office man was doubly
reinforced. The front-office job was a "Jew's job,"
which had nothing to do with industrial realities; not
even engineers and draftsmen were credited with the
fundamental knowledge which could be gained only
by the man who was working directly with the tools.
Whenever any hitch in the program caused expensive
errors or delayed schedules, it was always "those pencil
pushers" who were blamed. In the outfitting of a type
of ship unfamiliar in this particular shipyard some
difficulties arose which were traced eventually to dis-

crepancies in the blueprints. For days thereafter the workers indulged themselves in flinging insults at the front office. "Those blockheads with the pencils and the blueprints," an electrician angrily exclaimed, "don't know a damn thing about how a ship is actually put together. All they know is the names, and when it comes to attaching the names to the places where they belong, they're no handier at it than a blindfolded kid trying to pin the tail on the donkey."

The entire white-collar group, especially the feminine typists, secretaries, and file clerks who flocked through the front offices like so many chattering, brightly colored birds, aroused the same reaction. Although they could claim none of the power which excited mingled fear and hatred, they were believed to hold themselves superior to the rough-handed, dirty toilers in the crafts, and on this score were resented. They were, furthermore, accused of being bootlickers and the "little whores of wealth" who were all bent on marrying the boss's son or, as the next best opportunity for personal gain, on sleeping with the boss. In this attitude could be seen some of the anger of a simple man whose daughter, scorning the honest rudeness of the patriarchal hearth, has chosen to pursue the gauds of the traveling salesman. The occasional union-conscious worker had an additional charge to bring against the entire white-collar group, since their resistance to union-

ization was notorious: in trying to improve the poor
conditions of their work by toadying to the boss they
were believed to injure the cause of all labor.

The group of the educated, the academicians and
professionals, were yet another object of the envy, resentment, and contempt which possessors of superior
economic and social status customarily aroused. As an
academician, the evidences of whose education were
not to be concealed entirely by the most diligent appli-
cation of shipyard camouflage, I was myself directly
and personally involved in this particular complex of
hostilities. For a clear understanding of these attitudes,
the fact must be considered that the shipyard group represented a remarkably low level of educational achievement. With the influx of Negroes and Okies from the
rural South and Southwest this level was undoubtedly
reduced from that which would have obtained for prewar employees in the same industry; although an exact
figure was not available to me, it probably stood at
the fifth or sixth grade. But even among the products
of the cities and of regions indubitably rich in educational resources, experience with the mysteries of high
school was none too common, and graduation from the
secondary level was a marked exception. Most of the
older craftsmen of my acquaintance, in keeping with
the apparent code for their generation and status, had
left school at the end of the eighth grade; many of

the younger workers, especially the men, had evaded the truant officer and entered full-time employment at the age of fifteen or sixteen. But if secondary education was exceptional among shipyard workers, higher education was almost nonexistent. In two years I met among the ordinary craftsmen only a handful who had ever been to college.

Lack of opportunity was, of course, the primary explanation for the extremely low educational level of the Southern and Southwestern contingent of shipyard workers. Work in cotton fields in the spring and fall, lack of shoes or needed transportation in the winter, or similar limitations, had kept most Southern Negroes and the Okies from attending school regularly or long in their growing years. "Somehow in our family," an Oklahoman told me, "us young 'uns never managed to get out of that old fourth grade. There was always too much else for us to do, to take our schooling regular like we should." But also, in large part, the educational deficiencies of the shipyard workers were explained by the absence from the philosophy of the great mass of American workers of a tradition which would encourage scholastic endeavor to the exclusion of other and more immediately profitable use of time. Many of them consciously chose not to continue their schooling beyond a minimum level, even when they might have done so without hardship. One keen-minded Californian who was under thirty told me he had quit school at the age of fifteen. "I could have finished high school," he said; "my dad even kind of wanted me to go to college. But when I saw all the other fellows with their girl friends and their cars and lots of money, I couldn't wait any longer, so I got a job." He admitted, however, that with greater wisdom had come regret, and that he would try to prevent his son from committing the same error.

Rare among shipyard workers was any such statement of regret for missed opportunities of youth. Perhaps the regret existed, but if so it was concealed by an enthusiastic rendition of the "sour grapes" routine. That education should extend past the acquisition of the bare rudiments was generally questioned. Since the enjoyment of knowledge for its own sake lay quite outside the scope of shipyard comprehension, the only question asked of secondary and higher education was whether it paid cash returns. The answer was usually that it did not. I myself supplied the object lesson. In spite of my education I had been able, presumably, to find no better job and could earn no more in wages than all the thousands around me who had never entered high school. No reply of mine, however patient, could allay the suspicion that I had simply thrown away my years of book learning in wanton laziness and self-indulgence. The failures of educated men in handling practical affairs were greatly relished. "I knew a fellow once who went to college," a worker told me, triumphantly, "and he ended up a good-for-nothing and finally landed in jail." The consensus obviously was that the best possible educational course for their sons to follow was that which they themselves had set; schooling beyond the eighth grade was unnecessary, and beyond high school it was positively foolish and pernicious.

Except for the rare worker who had some inkling of the recent achievements of research laboratories, adoration of the physical scientist, supposedly omnipresent in American culture, had not penetrated to the shipyard level. Even the doctor, the popular representative of scientific method whose technique lies within the grasp of the savage mind, was not considered worthy of any special regard by the shipyard worker, who saw in him more the extortioner of fees than the patient ministrant to human needs. Every old wife was ready to challenge his authority with her own pet remedies, and the quacks of near-by communities, with their displays of pickled tapeworms and multicolored panaceas, throve on shipyard dollars. Although the engineer who worked directly with the men as acting foreman was sometimes generously conceded a deeper insight into the problem of shipbuilding than the simple workman's, the professionals of the front offices were credited with no knowledge which the worker could not duplicate or often exceed.

More theoretical disciplines than engineering and medicine, including the research aspects of the physical sciences, were altogether beyond concern or understanding, and were dismissed as of no consequence to the lives of ordinary men. I once tried to describe my own field of study to a not incurious listener, who gave heed as sympathetically as he could. I was interested, I said, in the study of society and its changes, and I related what this interest implied in terms of the specific problems which I sought to investigate and possibly to solve. "Oh, you mean," he exclaimed, as a look of enlightenment suffused his face, "you mean that you're a social worker," and carefully though I explained and illustrated, I never got past this initial road block in his comprehension. The value of a broad, objective social view was without significance to the average shipyard worker, who did not question his own analysis of social issues or feel the need of turning to a more expert source for information and advice. His prejudices were his facts. The opinions of a person educated in this field were discredited, rather than strengthened, by the background of study from which they came.

Ignorance was the seed and root of the shipyard skepticism concerning science and the value of higher learning, and ignorance was the only earth in which this skepticism could flourish. But the ignorance of the shipyard worker was no mere absence or lack or vacuum; it was itself a positive and militant principle, which fought off all efforts to uproot or strangle it. The educated man was not only undervalued and ridiculed; he was also actively resisted and resented. I used all my social skill in trying to keep the stigma of education from denying me the sympathy or affection of my fellow workers. "Gee, you talk funny," one girl said to me soon after I started work at the yards, "like you were stuck-up or something." Yet I never escaped completely from the suspicion and disapproval that my education evoked. I was not an exceptional case whose difficulties were perhaps to be attributed to peculiarities of personality existing apart from the acquisition of a degree or two. The foreman of one of the machine shops told me that he always instructed any young fellows who, fresh from a year or two of college engineering, came there for practical experience, not to mention their background. "The boys won't like you," he would explain to them, "if they find out you've been to college. They'll play tricks on you and make your life as miserable as they can."

Education, particularly higher education, still retained in shipyard opinion its feudalistic character as a useless mark of caste and privilege. It was conceived to be as much a matter of conspicuous display and unnecessary adornment as the delicate accomplishments of the traditional lily-fingered ladies who "toil not, neither do they spin" and who therefore could afford to become learned. Like sables and fine jewels, any but basic education was assumed to have no function in the environment of the ordinary man, and the worker who had achieved more than the scholastic average was likely to be assailed as pretending to a status to which he had no legitimate claim. Had the shipyard worker been confident that through education he might attain the position to which learning was an incidental adorn- ment, and had he been sure that the long years of sec- ondary and college training were indeed the arduous but unerring path to greater income and privilege, his attitude toward the whole issue would have been differ- ent. But such confidence was by no means his; education was, to him, no more than an evidence of privilege, and not the means by which it might be gained.

The more deeply the shipyard concepts of privilege and the possessors of privilege are penetrated, the more clearly one sees that, while the possessors were ma- ligned, privilege itself was never genuinely a subject of dispute. That no vision of an equalitarian society was abroad in the shipyards to challenge customary distinctions was clearly demonstrated to me in a dis- cussion of the preamble to the Declaration of Independ- ence. "We hold these truths to be self-evident," I quoted to a shipyard group, "that all men are created equal," and then I asked what this fine phrase conveyed to them.

"Well," remarked one sharp-witted man, "men may be created equal like the fellow who wrote that Declaration says, but they sure as hell ain't born that way, and so far as I can see, no bunch of fancy words is going to change the world and make all poor men rich." Unquestioning, as if it were the immutable laws of the universe which he recited, he proceeded to consider the various differences of power and privilege which divided men. "There are people, and you know it," he concluded, "who wouldn't even let such bums as us come through any door in their houses except the back one, and I guess if we lived in the houses and they worked in the shipyards, we'd feel and do the very same."

For all the shipyard worker's loudly asserted pride in his way of life and the work he was doing, he was essentially not proud or satisfied. Along with his acceptance of the hierarchical society as natural, eternal, and inevitable, he also accepted its scale of values, and felt in his heart that work with the hands and the useful toil of the wage earner were less honorable and less pleasurable than the dilettantism of leisured wealth. One shipyard worker expressed what was no doubt a common view when he remarked, "I never really wanted to be a workingman; I was just forced into it." Out of the very discontent with his place in society and weariness with the endless round of ordinary tasks sprang much of the ardor of the shipyard worker's defensiveness, and the distance between doubt of himself and aggressive contempt for the Jew, the front-office boss, and the educated man was actually not so great as it might at first glance appear to be. His real dream was not of the society in which the dignity of toil is recognized and all men are as brothers. It was rather the dream of the ship come in, of the oil gusher miraculously spouting in his back yard, of the long-lost and fabulously rich uncle's sudden demise; it was the dream of unexpected wealth which would waft him out of the dull world of the workingman and into the realm of mansions, limousines, and servants. It was the dream of "easy street," which, if its reality could once be achieved, would end forever the tedious necessity of rising to the jangling summons of a Big Ben and of stumbling out, lunch box under arm, into the dark, cold morning. "I'm too old now to get very far, myself," confided a shipyard father, "but I just keep praying that my boys will have an easier time than I have had and that when they grow up they'll be able to live like gentlemen."

In contemporary society, the shipyard worker was keen-eyed enough to observe, wealth was the indispensable basis of privilege; it was the solid pillar about which the other attributes of the gentleman and the gentleman's life twined like decorative vines. And, suitably enough, the shipyard worker had an insatiable interest in the means by which wealth might be attained. The workingman was well acquainted with useful money, the dollars and cents of his weekly pay check which he had earned with his own toil, the steady income matched by an equally steady outgo. The approach to wealth lay quite apart from toil, wages, and bills. For wealth was the excess beyond necessity, the brimming pot of gold which never could be spent, the marvelous hoard which the miser might achieve by a lifetime of penny-pinching, but which oftener was spilled suddenly from the buckets on fortune's wheel.

Speculation was always busy around the few old bachelors who, with their stringy fingers and unpatched clothes, plodded to their shipyard work each morning as they had done through fifty-odd years of various employments. It was commonly believed that many of them, lacking wife and child to drain off their resources, had amassed large sums of money and persisted in working only because of the inflexibility of their miser's habits. Such men, who, though they gathered wealth, did not extract from it its precious substance of idleness and display, were not admired or emulated by the shipyard audience. But their supposed riches gave rise to splendid fancies about "what I would do if I could get my hands on the old fellow's pile." "Gosh, you sure must have a full sock hidden in your mattress," a worker teasingly remarked to one of these reputed Silas

Marners. "Come on, Dad, and tell us where you keep
it, so somebody at least can get the good from it."

I met only a few men who, eschewing both the miser's
passion and the general resignation concerning the pursuit of wealth, plotted a course of thrift and investment
which they hoped would lift them to the position in
society they coveted. Home ownership was their preliminary step, and those who owned a home—among
the uprooted, underprivileged thousands of the shipyards these were a very small minority—expressed
pride in their achievement. But the traditional spirit of
individual enterprise was adequately shown by only
one of all the shipyard workers I knew well. He was
young and vigorous, his father had previously gained
a measure of respectability, and he had a plan to take
himself further yet. He owned his home already, and
would start a small business after the war. Meanwhile,
the shipyard job was both a haven from the draft and
a chance to add to his postwar capital. "Every month I
put at least a hundred bucks into the bank," he proudly
told me. To make additional saving possible, he slaved
through months of overtime and Sunday work, denied
himself his week of vacation, and, despite his occasional hangovers and winter colds, doggedly came to
work with almost fanatical regularity. I once inquired
what overwhelming purpose drove him on. "Don't think
I work like this because I love it," he answered; "but

I keep watching those figures growing in my bank book, and I keep looking ahead to the time when I am old and I can loaf and enjoy myself like a rich man every day. The way I see it, that's worth working for."

For the most part, however, the shipyard worker had no faith in his ability to plod to wealth and idleness. Wealth, he believed, was neither to be earned nor patiently entreated, and it had little to do with talent. Wealth was either, like the Jew's ill-gotten riches, a product of cunning to which the worker denied his readiness to stoop, or, like a royal flush in poker, it merely came by chance to a few—a few who were no more deserving than himself—and was therefore quite beyond the reach of conscious planning or deliberate choice. Most wealthy people happened to be born to their desirable estate; others happened to stumble on good fortune, as witlessly as the child in the fairy story stumbles on a pot of gold. The corollary of this view, which was the secret of its charm and strength, was the stimulating promise that what had happened to others might with equal unpredictability and suddenness happen likewise to oneself. Thus the hard substances of fact, the inevitable sequences which in nature bind a cause to its effect, and the pitiless laws of contemporary economy which tend visibly to perpetuate the poor in their poverty and the wealthy in their riches, were all pushed aside. For dominant in the mind and reasoning of the average shipyard worker was the gambler's ever-vigorous hope that the next turn of the wheel, the next throw of the dice, would reveal that chance which meant the conquest of the world.

Because the shipyard worker never felt himself to be altogether and irrevocably excluded from the world of wealth and the status that wealth bestowed, neither was he altogether ready to repudiate the hierarchical system toward whose pinnacle he looked with longing eyes. His resentment against the possessors of privilege was therefore never broadened into a resentment against privilege itself. So far as he entertained the hope that through a lucky shift in circumstance he too might some day live in the mansions of the mighty and eat his food from the finest Dresden plates, thus far was he discouraged from any consistent or basic criticism of the social hierarchy and its rigidities. Much as he complained against the surfeit of the rich and against his own insufficiencies, there was always this gambler's vision of the unlimited possibilities of chance to frustrate the formation of a stable rebellious attitude.

The triumph which the shipyard worker pictured for himself, the mere imagined occurrence of which was enough to quiet discontent and lull the pains of life, was the triumph of an individual chosen by chance from all the world. Since it implied and accepted the disappointment of the mass of men as a concomitant of the happiness of one, it was, in truth, the triumph of a gambler whose winnings are inevitably a compound of the losses of many others. I never knew a shipyard worker to display moral revulsion at this factor in his concepts. All those with whom I discussed the subject blandly viewed the phenomena of competition between individuals for social place and the balancing of the success of a few against the failure of the many as the natural elements of a cruel and bloody universe. "It's dog eat dog, and the strongest gets the most in this man's world," one worker told me; "it's always been that way, and that's the way, I guess, it's always bound to be."

The majority of shipyard workers appeared to settle quietly into acceptance of the inevitability of conflict and the unequal distribution of the world's good things, and limited their expression of the prevalent cynicism concerning man and his society to minimum measures of defense of their own interests. They tended to be suspicious of the motives and behavior of other men, and were quick to scent some evidence of corruption in every instance of another man's achievement. They contributed their share to distrust of the wealthy and resentment against the privileged, but they formed no plan of compensating aggression. A few among the group I knew, however, who were either more ambitious or more cantankerous than the average, transformed their conviction of the inherent selfish-

ness of man from a passive belief into an evangelistic
creed. They often took pains to tell me I was foolish
in contributing such unrewarded services as I performed for the union, my political party, or any cause
which currently had my support. "It's not natural for
a person to work the way you do just for the sake of
doing good and helping others," declared one man
who saw in my small deeds the acme of self-sacrifice.
"Everybody else is out for himself and for what he
can get from the world, and they'll not thank you for
behaving different."

Of all the discourses and comments I heard on the
subject, I particularly remember one long, ardent lecture delivered to me by a man who was undoubtedly
the most unpleasant and malignant person I ever met
in the yards. This composite of almost every form of
legal human viciousness was a man in his late sixties
who, after a childhood of melodramatic misery in the
South, had grubbed his way to financial security; in
the classic manner of the miser, he planned to work
to his dying day lest he spend a penny of his capital.
He was boastful, aggressive, and the loud-mouthed
carrier of all the prevailing prejudices. As a petty
boss, he tyrannized over his inferiors and toadied
shamelessly to his superiors; he hated mankind indis-
criminately, and mankind, for its part, spared no love
on him. In an expansive mood he condescended to

give me some advice. "You're young," he said, "and pretty smart, I think. Now, if you watch your chance, you can really get ahead in the world and make a lot of money. All you have to do is to think of yourself first in every situation, always to think of yourself before you consider anybody else, for in the long run it's only yourself that counts." He concluded his advice in the habitual manner of the old who prescribe for the young. "If I had known when I was young like you," he assured me, "everything about the dumbness of other people and the tricks a smart man can play on them that I know now, I'd have been a millionaire two or three times over."

The exaltation of personal advantage and aggressive individualism almost completely inhibited the judgment of human conduct, outside the narrow realm of friend-to-friend relationships, on the basis of general standards of morality. I can scarcely recall a single dispute in which appeal was made to abstract concepts of right and justice. Except for the occasional Bible-quoter, such concepts had little meaning, and seldom were enlisted even to provide added support for conclusions. One man stated his entire moral philosophy this way: "What's good is what's good for me, and what's bad is what hurts me or what keeps from me the things I want to have. It doesn't take much living on this earth to figure that one out."

Under the influence of this view, judgments concerning actions and policies on the individual and the social level alike tended to be reduced to the small change of opportunism. Attitudes, principles, and convictions of all sorts were seen as the legitimate concomitants of position in life and status in society. During the presidential election campaign of 1944, for instance, it was generally conceded that a voter's registration as a Republican or a Democrat depended primarily upon whether or not he had money in the bank and whether he had an interest in the welfare of the business community as distinguished from the community of workers. One minor boss whose wages exceeded the average was uncertain which party should have his loyalty. His brothers, he said, had shifted, with the recent increase of their incomes and the value of their property, from Democrat to Republican, and he was not altogether sure whether his position and his bank account were now reason enough for his making the change, too. When, as a partisan myself, I chided his opportunism, he complacently replied, "Well, it's loyalty enough for me to stand by the bunch that pays me off the best."

The philosophy of individualism and opportunism was a further factor in the discouragement of fundamental criticism of the injustices of a hierarchical society. According to the principles of judgment which this philosophy established, it was possible to resent particular instances of discrimination and to take exception to the current possessors of the power to discriminate and oppress, since they constituted encroachments and limitations upon the personal freedoms of the underprivileged individual. But it was not possible to go past this point to the condemnation of the entire concept of discrimination and the whole system of privilege. Hope of such extension of petty resentments of specific grievances into a broad and high-principled rebellion was effectively blocked by the shoulder-shrugging admission, typical of the workers and the opportunistic outlook which they cherished, that if they were rich and had the necessary power they would build against others the same walls of exclusion that now confronted and obstructed them.

Some aspects of the philosophy of individualism, however, seemed to make a positive contribution to the dignity and status of the worker. When one considers what mixtures of adult comprehension and childish barbarism are so many of the ideologies of man, it is not surprising that the very attitudes which made for ruthless opportunism also produced pride and healthy independence. Conscious though the shipyard workers were of the inferiority of their economic and social status, I never knew a white man among them who was essentially servile or broken in spirit. Their pride in themselves and their capacities was strong. To the de-

gree that wealth and privilege were the province of the
wicked and the Jews, the very poverty of the workers
could be considered a badge of honor. Working people
were generally assumed, moreover, to have potentiali-
ties of leadership and achievement which only special
circumstances revealed. In support of this position one
shipyard worker pointed out to me how many workingmen, "just plain Joes like any of us here," had
become widely acclaimed heroes in response to the challenge of the war. "You can't know what's in a guy until
you give him a chance to show it," he concluded, "and
outside of something unusual like a war, most of us
working fellows never get the chance." Another man
thought that, for all the ridicule that was heaped on shipyard workers and their presumed stupidities, "they're
really just as smart as any other bunch. All people," he
continued, "have some talent hidden in them somewhere; the lucky ones among them get an opportunity
to develop it and use it; the rest of us never do." Thus
by the rugged confidence in his individual worth the
shipyard worker was enabled, in the arena of his own
mind at any rate, to stand up before the rich and powerful and to assert, with sufficient vigor for his own complete belief, that he had no sense of inward or natural
inferiority.

In the foregoing discussion a long and devious course
has been undertaken in the search for such evidence

of consciousness of economic class as might exist among a group of shipyard workers. And now, at the end, the evidence is revealed to be no more than an assemblage of shreds and tags, uncertain in its beginnings and emerging nowhere as an entire and identifiable form. It has been seen, of course, that the shipyard worker typically disliked possessors of extreme wealth, whom he tended to equate with the malicious figure of the Jew. He also nourished a feeling of bitterness toward those who had secured the appurtenances of wealth, such as a degree of authority or power and a superior education. But at no time did this resentment against the rich man, the boss, and the educated man—all, in the shipyard view, one person, whose essential quality was the ownership of wealth—evolve into resentment against a distinct class of exploiters or expropriators and against the hierarchical system which sustained them. The shipyard worker was withheld from complete development of class consciousness, as a type of social unity, not only by his initial failure to formulate specific antagonisms into an integrated policy of rebellion, but also by his failure to concede the common character of his interests and those of other workingmen. It was as a uniquely fortunate individual, and not as a member of a class, that he hoped for deliverance from the limiting conditions of his social and economic status. The elements of class consciousness were present in the shipyard worker's attitudes, and the practical conditions for the existence of the concept were active in his environment, but the overwhelming weight of his accustomed thought and the largest part of the traditions by which he lived still supported a philosophy of self-sufficiency and competitive individualism.

SHIPYARD NATIONALISM

✤ By VIRTUE of his residence in the world the shipyard worker was confronted by the claims of even larger unities than those which have already been considered; for he was not only a member of a labor union or a representative of an economic class, but also a citizen of a continent-spanning nation very great in productive capacity and with traditions that were yet vigorous, young, and compelling. For all that such affiliation might mean in terms of loyalty, national pride, and a sense of solidarity with his fellows the shipyard worker was an American. He was part, furthermore, of a nation at war. The very industry in which he worked was sustained by the war, and in every detail of his daily toil he was reminded of the dangers that surrounded his homeland and of its consequent demands upon him for service and devotion. The appeal to national unity, as definitely as the steel hulls he was building, loomed before him and beckoned him to a continent-wide, and ultimately a world-wide, field of interest. It remains to be seen how far and in what manner the shipyard worker, bounded by his various provincialisms, chose to respond.

A type of patriotism, simple as the schoolchild's morning pledge of allegiance to the flag, did indeed stir in the depths of his nature and became overt upon the

proper ceremonial occasion. When the shipyard band
closed its noontime concerts with "The Star-Spangled
Banner," almost all the men within hearing distance
rose to their feet and took off their hats, and here and
there a tear was wiped away by a work-hardened hand.
Otherwise, the shipyard sense of loyalty to the nation
was almost inarticulate. The only enthusiastic American
whom I met among my colleagues was a woman, natively a Greek, whose newly acquired citizenship was
already a source of pride to her; but "these Americans,"
she told me, "don't take the interest in their country that
they should. Maybe if they lived a while in the poor
village where I was born, they'd know what a good thing
they have got and work to keep it so or even make it
better."

The war, of course, was the major expression of the
nation's existence and purpose while I was in the shipyard. Like all wars, this conflict, in the very process of
segregating the enemy, tended to amalgamate the disparate elements of the home community. But the war
also demanded unusual sacrifices of the citizen, even to
the sacrifice of life itself, and thus the intensified unity
which the threat of the enemy provided was partly negated by the additional strains placed upon the loyalty
of the individual. Most workers in the shipyard responded well to the minor sacrifices. More than half of
them consistently pledged at least ten per cent of their

pay checks to the purchase of bonds; many, conscious, to be sure, that they were making a good investment as well as a patriotic gesture, bought bonds to the limit of their financial capacity. In spite of a suspicion that the real beneficiaries of organized charity were the organizers, response to the annual appeals of the War Chest were substantial. The workers were generous blood donors, too, and this contribution must be doubly weighed in view of their difficulties in finding a chance to go to the blood-donating center and their tiring and unhealthful work.

Wartime economic controls were accepted without complaint and were even actively supported by the majority of workers, but since most of the controls were beneficial to them the element of sacrifice was not large. Rent and food-price ceilings, for instance, were wholly advantageous to a city-dwelling, transient group who neither owned their homes nor produced their food. Food rationing similarly helped workers whose level of income was so low that they were unable to hoard even had they wished to. "Sure, I'm for rationing," a woman worker said; "before they rationed meat I'd go to the butcher shop on my way home from work and there wouldn't be nothing left for me and the old man and the kids to eat. Now, I can count on getting just as much as anybody else does." Gasoline rationing, on the other hand, was not consistently approved; in fact, the need of it was widely questioned, and though extensive dealing with the black market was beyond the pocket-books of most, little moral stigma attached to it.

The ceiling on wages, while much discussed by those who were interested in the problems of labor, did not particularly concern the shipyard group as a whole. Some of this indifference was no doubt due to the fact that wage rates in the shipyards were among the nation's highest and seemed all the higher to the many new-comers accustomed to much less. The boom was too short for these workers to become so contemptuous of their pay checks as to clamor for more. The general con-tentment with the conditions of their work also helped them to accept the regulations by which they were bound to their jobs. Although an occasional worker, either from wanderlust or from dislike for his boss, might try to break free and complain of the red tape which held him, most of the workers, recognizing a good thing when they saw it, were content to stay put.

For the majority of workers the war was an experi-ence of opportunity rather than limitation. Their war-time income was larger than ever before, and they ate more abundantly and lived more agreeably. The men of draft age were also aware that every day in the ship-yard was a day not spent in a barracks or a foxhole, and were properly grateful. In comparison with such bless-ings, the immediate source of which was the shipyards, the compensating tribute of the wartime income taxes seemed of little moment; when March 15 approached, most workers, making no effort to avoid the burden, passively consigned the data about their income and dependents to the professional "figurers" in the brightly painted kiosks set up by the shipyard gates.

Little of the war was to be noted in the worker's common talk. Although newspaper headlines constantly told of battles fought, ships torpedoed, and cities bombed, days passed in the shipyards when I heard no reference to these events. I knew one worker, to be sure, who kept maps of the important battle fronts pinned above his bench and traced on them the progress of the armies of the Allies; but he was a foreigner whose English was scarcely understandable and who was thought crazy by his fellows. A placid ignorance enveloped the strange place names of the war, and the conflict assumed an air of vast distance and unreality. Many workers resisted discussion of the war as they might of death. "I don't like to think about the war," was the remark that often terminated consideration of the state of world affairs. The horror of modern warfare was seldom confronted face to face; guns were put in place on the decks with as little thought of their ultimate purpose as if they had been winches or extra booms.

Indifference to the war was not, however, altogether a result of the tendency to shrink from unpleasant reali-

ties. Another and perhaps more fundamental cause was
an undeviating confidence that America would quickly
be the victor. Faith in the capacity of "our side" to win
easily in both the Pacific and Atlantic theaters was an
almost tiresomely constant attitude which no defeats
or delays could weaken and which blossomed into jubi-
lation with every triumph. No shipyard worker of my
experience ever considered for a moment that America
might lose. There was a large segment of opinion which
already had brought the war to a triumphant close in
Europe with the first landings in Sicily in 1943. After
D-Day and the pursuit across France in the late summer
of 1944, the conviction was universal that the Germans
would drop their weapons and surrender before the
mighty American onslaught by the middle of the next
week or at the latest by the following Monday. One bit
of mystic nonsense gained a large audience of the gul-
lible in late August, 1944. Manipulation of data on the
various leaders of the warring nations, such as their
birth dates and their years in power, led to a prediction
that the European conflict would draw to its close at
2:00 P.M., September 7. When this day passed, others
were selected with equal confidence, if not with equal
unanimity, until at last November 11 emerged the fa-
vorite. All this time, I seemed to be alone in advocating
patience and greater modesty of expectation; and even
I was shortly reduced to silence when I discovered that

what was meant for wise counsel was interpreted as close to traitorousness. "Are you a communist or something," one shipyard worker inquired angrily, "that you keep telling us the war ain't over yet?"

The obverse side of wartime patriotism, the due and proper hatred of the enemy, was also well developed—though in an unbalanced manner, since the German enemy never aroused the same fever of vengeance as did the Japanese. Anger against the Germans was mainly channeled, moreover, toward the single leader or the single group deemed to have misguided a worthy folk, but anger against the Japanese was directed against a nation and a people, and with the publicizing of every new Japanese atrocity the bloodthirsty shouted for the annihilation of the foe, down to the veriest babe. The geographical location of the shipyards in part explained this preference in hatred, since the war in the Pacific naturally seemed closer and more real to those who dwelt upon the ocean's shores and could imagine the lurking of Japanese submarines in their harbors; but the more basic factor was probably the conjunction of a national and a racial antagonism which mutually reinforced each other.

A simple pride in the nation's vigor, certainty of its victory, and a rousing hatred of its enemies—such was the substance of shipyard patriotism. But although this patriotism had its area of generosity and self-sacrifice, it also had its limitations. I met no man who had entered the industry for patriotic reasons alone. Indeed, most of the young men quite openly admitted that they were in the yards to escape the draft. They would make every legal effort—extralegal too, perhaps—to avoid induction. When the last dodge had been exhausted and the call to duty finally came, a man was expected, according to the code, to go with fair good humor, while the commiserations of the luckier workers followed after. One young quarterman whose attitude was typical approached each date for the renewal of his "essential" status with a mixture of dread and resignation that was amusing to behold. He ran frantically to his foreman and the superintendent of his craft to assure himself of their continued support, and talked fervently to his colleagues of his family's need of him and his civilian income. But after the third or fourth recurrence of this crisis he finally said wearily, "Jeez, I almost wish they'd get me this time so I wouldn't have to worry any more."

No shipyard worker whom I knew left his job to enlist. The volunteer was scoffed at as a fool or disliked for setting a bad precedent. I was once witness to a protracted argument by the friends of a young man who, as the result of a series of personal frustrations and an unsatisfied thirst for adventure, had determined to join the Merchant Marine. "You're just being a sucker for all the flag waving that's going on these days," chided one of his counselors, and another reminded him of the income he would lose, of his isolation from normal life, and of the dangers he would face if he were to pursue so foolish a course. "And how's your old lady going to feel if you pick up and leave her alone with the kid that way?" the first friend questioned. "For myself, I wouldn't blame her if she found another guy while you were gone." The strenuous appeals had the calculated effect, and, freshly reminded of the paramount importance of his familial duties, he withdrew from the excitement of a life upon the sea and turned to sober planning for the purchase of a home. In the pursuit of this second venture, incidentally, which lacked all taint of self-sacrificing devotion to a cause, the young man's friends were endlessly helpful and encouraging.

In the eyes of the workers, the tasks of the shipyards themselves assumed no special urgency because of their significance to the total war effort. Despite the occasional outburst of official cajolery, no newer or broader appeal than the ancient traditions of craftsmanship was effectively evoked to bestir the workers to more proficient toil. Indeed, most of them confessed with a disgusted shrug that they had never worked less proficiently. An atmosphere of lassitude floated like a heavy vapor over the yards, and everywhere was evidence of an incredible waste of time. Scarcely more than half the average worker's day was consistently occupied with

productive tasks. The tedium of the remaining hours
was relieved by various standard devices for killing
time. Groups of gossips were clustered everywhere;
newspapers were surreptitiously brought out and read;
and in the secluded corners of the hulls and shops the
dice throwers and poker players busily pursued their
pastimes. At times when work was especially slack I
have myself stood guard at the door of a tool shack,
ready to warn of the approach of a superintendent or a
front-office boss, while for day after day nine or ten
lesser bosses and workmen played poker with passionate absorption.

The source of this disorder, however, was not so much
in the workers' attitudes as in the inability or unwilling-
ness of the shipyard management to control and direct
the sprawling mass of the industry; here was the primary factor that choked any incipient growth of patriotic enthusiasm, poisoned the craftsman's instincts, and
stimulated a cancerous spread of cynicism about the
job, the war, and the state of the nation. The workers
generally believed that, because of the company's contract, speed or low cost of construction was not an object,
since the greater the cost of the ship the larger the profit
for the company. "The front office should care if we sit
around all day," observed one worker blandly, "so long
as they get their cut nice and regular from the government!" The workers adjusted to the inefficiency, but

most of them did so with a measure of reluctance. "I've worked hard all my life," a craftsman told me, "and when I first came to the shipyards I expected to do the same. Now that I've been here for two years, I wonder if I'll ever be able to do an honest day's work again."

Many another was vaguely troubled at the ease with which he earned his wages, and it was a standard joke among the men that they should walk backward to the pay window. The hours between useful tasks were little welcomed by the workers. The usual pastimes palled after a while, and boredom settled like a heavy weight upon them. I never heard a worker protest that he had too much to do, but time and again I have seen men come to their bosses to complain that they weren't busy enough or were doing useless and misdirected tasks. In slack periods it was painful to watch the men fret and wander aimlessly from place to place. "Christ! I can't stand no more of this," an idle pipefitter exclaimed. "I need the money they pay me here, but I don't need it bad enough to keep me standing around and watching the clock all day." He relieved his feelings by spending the rest of the week at home. This impatience had little to do with the war, of course; it was due rather to the tradition of the workingman that wages should be a rightfully earned reward. I remember only one time when the war added poignancy to the frustration of honest desire to work. It was the morning of D-Day, and it happened that

just then there was an unusual production blockage at
Moore Dry Dock. A group of men were standing about
in the weak morning light and discussing the mighty
event of which the headlines had just told them. As the
group grew silent and slowly began to disperse, one
man among them looked at the cluttered deck on which
they stood and remarked, "I'd sure as hell like to do
something for those boys over there, if only there was
something I could find to do."

The issues of the war, other than those expressed in
the simple terms of hatred of Hitler or the Japanese,
were almost completely lacking in meaning to the average shipyard worker. Positive objectives or negative
provocations were not pursued beyond the sneak attack
on Pearl Harbor, the dastardly designs of the Germans
and the Japanese upon American interests, and the supposed obliquities of the Japanese as a people. Nazism
and Fascism were mere labels, seldom used, having
only the sketchiest meaning. They were vaguely associated with violence, dictatorship, and a kind of gangster
rule, but their significance as a whole had hardly
enough solidity or emotional impact to motivate a minor
street brawl, let alone a world war. The phrases which
presumably described the positive goals for which the
nation fought, the Four Freedoms and the Atlantic Char-
ter, for example, were passed over as so much pious
patter from a Sunday school.

More than indifference was involved in this response to the ideology of war; an active skepticism also confronted such compacts and charters, the real function of which, it was assumed, was to obscure with fine talk a naked selfishness and lust for power which lay beneath. Wars were not fought for high ideals and splendid goals, nor were they conducted with consideration for the welfare of the workingman. Wars were fought by the poor, but it was the rich who made them and used them as devices for the enlargement of their influence. "This war is just a businessman's affair," one worker said, "and those guys who make the profits out of it are going to try to keep it going as long as they can." He argued that the war was started to relieve the pressure of unemployment, partly through the stimulus which wars always provided for industrial activity and partly through the expedient of killing off the world's excessive population; another of the major purposes of war, he pointed out, was to quiet the common people and their threats of rebellion against the rich and powerful by distracting them with more compelling interests, fears, and hatreds. "It wasn't Hitler and Hirohito by themselves who began this war," he concluded; "it was the big fellows all over the world who wanted the war, and so they got it." A minor boss had a more derisive view. "Sure I'm in the shipyards to avoid the draft," he loudly announced, "and I'm not buying any war bonds,

either. Let the suckers do the fighting and the dying and
the paying through the nose so a few more millionaires
can have their marble swimming pools. I got better
things to do with my money and my life." He and others
like him were convinced that the attack on Pearl Harbor
was arranged by businessmen and politicians as an excuse for a war, and they reduced the war and all its
ideology to a program of deceit and trickery practiced
by the rich and idle upon the poor. Such statements as
theirs were of course extreme, but skepticism was so
widespread as to allow public pronouncement of them
without fear of censure.

Some among the shipyard analysts distinguished between one group of national leaders, the sincerity of
whose aims they trusted in the war, and other groups
which they viewed with persistent and unrelieved cynicism. These distinctions became particularly sharp and
obvious at the time of the presidential election in the
fall of 1944. Intensely partisan Democrats, for instance, of which there were a fair number among the
workers, defended the current administration's conduct
of the war and predicted all the horrors of corruption
should power be seized by the opposing party. "What
I like about this war," said one ardent Democrat, "is
that rich men's sons are dying in it alongside the sons
of ordinary people. But if the Republicans win out in
the election, then it'll be a war like any other, run for

the benefit of the rich and at the expense of the working guys." The Republicans in the yards, who compensated for their minority status by increased vehemence, attributed the whole disaster of the war to the machinations of the Democratic party and were confident of early victory and peace with a change in leadership.

The campaign, like the war, was peculiarly suited to the revelation of shipyard attitudes toward the nation. As a partisan and a registrar of voters, I was both interested in these attitudes and favorably situated for observing them. In the spring and autumn drives I registered nearly a thousand workers at Moore Dry Dock—by dint of extreme effort on my part. I was compelled to seek the voters out; seldom, if ever, did they seek me. Approximately three-fourths of them chose the Democratic party, some making this selection because they were from the Southwest, others feeling either a personal loyalty to President Roosevelt or a vague sense, which stemmed in part from experience with the relief projects of the depression, that the Democrats held the interests of the poor man in somewhat greater esteem than the Republicans. Among them were some who took their politics very seriously and felt that the welfare of all workingmen was at stake. I remember one old craftsman who for the last few weeks before the fateful date fretted anxiously as if awaiting a verdict of great importance to his personal happiness. "There are too many numbskulls around who are sure to vote for that Republican," he complained. "I just can't understand how fellows who've worked with their hands for twenty-five years, and who ought to know what the score is, can be so dumb; but that's the way they are, and sometimes I think the situation's hopeless."

Political enthusiasts, however, were uncommon. Few among the workers, I had reason to believe, chose their party with any detailed understanding of issues or with any deep-seated convictions. They were indifferent and skeptical. When I approached with my pencil and registration blank, many were surprisingly reluctant to accept the opportunity afforded them. Some who openly expressed suspicion, I was able to persuade. One woman, however, remained beyond the reach of argument. She was from a small town in Missouri and was well into her fifties; she had never voted. "I never saw no point in voting," she declared. "All them politicians is as crooked as a cowpath, anyhow." She obviously felt ill at ease about any dealings with the machinery of state. "How do I know what'll happen to me," she asked, "if I put my name on that paper you're shoving at me? Maybe it'll cost me some money sometime." Even of those who registered, moreover, I was fully aware that less than half would vote. With more foundation in fact than I was willing to concede at the moment, one Republican worker, a minor boss, when confronted with the

Democratic trend of my registration record, observed, "Most of those ignorant working people wouldn't have bothered to register if you hadn't come along and pushed the blanks right under their noses; and they won't vote, either, unless somebody drives them to the polls in a limousine and feeds them a chicken dinner besides."

The Missouri woman's belief that all political leaders were corrupt was at the root of the shipyard indifference to political issues. Like union elections, national elections were skeptically deemed to have little bearing upon a worker's personal affairs. Politicians, of whatever party, were assumed to be grasping men whose protestations of interest in the welfare of the common man were so much honey spread to catch the flies. Few shipyard workers had faith in the publicized program of any political party, or gave ardent support to its endeavors.

Shipyard workers, moreover, since they reduced political issues to contests for power between competing groups, were impatient of interference in their private lives by political partisans. My efforts as a registrar were frequently resented, and some workers were sure that I was being paid well for my activities. "Well, girlie, maybe I'll do you a favor and sign up with you," was the typical and only partly humorous approach to registration. In this whole pattern of reluctance could be seen the conviction that the vote was not a device by which a man's opinion was effectively expressed, but was instead a gift which, after a lively and amusing contest among all possible recipients, was bestowed upon the candidate who had passed around the best cigars.

The shipyard worker emerges from this survey as neither nationally nor politically minded. To be sure, he felt a degree of identity with his nation and would have been deeply grieved had it lost the war, and he displayed no active hostility against the impositions of the state, which, in this time of peril, could reach down into the personal affairs of its citizens and demand the risk even of life itself. But his docile acceptance of the claims of his nation was undoubtedly far more the result of a consciousness of irresistible might before which the rebellion of the individual would be futile than the outcome of a positive sense of loyalty, alliance, or complete agreement. In actuality, the vast institutional entities of the nation and the state were alien to his real interests. He had neither confidence in his capacity even moderately to affect political policies, nor any awareness that his and his nation's destiny were intertwined. Indeed, since the destiny of the nation was conceived to be in the hands of men of power who pursued their selfish interests rather than the common good and who employed the machinery of the state to force conformity, the shipyard worker was even anxious to maintain the distance between himself and these agen-

cies of control. Though he was not actively hostile toward the nation's incursions into his private life, he
suspected its purposes, and though he was not rebellious
against the controls of the state, he chose not to participate in its affairs. Thus, like the labor union and the
economic class, the state and the nation failed to provide an institutional unity into which shipyard workers
might feel themselves absorbed.

Since widespread cynicism existed among the shipyard workers regarding the other than selfish aims of
their own nation at war, it could hardly be expected that
the stated motives of other nations fighting beside America would be accepted without emendation. The feeling
expressed toward Russia and Great Britain was almost
invariably antagonistic, only slightly less so than that
directed toward the European enemy. As viewed in relation to this antagonism, America was a nation which
lived in truth and fought an idealistic, self-sacrificing
war in order that other, more calculating and greedy
peoples might be saved from merited destruction. Pa-
tently, America was doing a job that England was too
proud and too effete to do for herself, and any tale that
American successes on a common front were greater
than British, or that American casualties were higher,
was evidence of the British plot into which America had
been dragged as a lamb to the slaughter. "We're doing
just what we did in the last war," one man said; "we're

saving Britain and her Empire with the blood of our boys." "Yeah, it's sure a swell kind of war," said another, "with England getting all the plums and us getting all the casualty lists." One woman, recently arrived from the Middle West, asserted her belief that since Hitler was the creature of Britain, built up, she declared, by British political and financial aid, Britain alone should dispose of him. "Instead of that," she angrily concluded, "it's America that's fighting Britain's war."

The full weight of anti-British opinion was revealed to me on one occasion when I challenged it. In the late summer of 1943, when American forces were struggling to survive at Salerno, I pointed out that the army which was moving to the rescue was a British army under British command. The first reaction to my facts was disbelief; the second was an angry attack on me and my doubtful patriotism. "If you're so blasted fond of the English," I was told, "why don't you go over to that country and settle down with them?"

The shipyard worker had other complaints to lodge against Great Britain; he saw it, in comparison with America, as a backward country whose institutions were notably disadvantageous to the workingman. Those few who knew directly, or indirectly through relatives, of the labor conditions in Great Britain were busy publicizers of the miseries and injustices from which they had escaped by the lucky chance of residence in another land. "My father," one son of an English immigrant remarked, "worked for fifty cents a day in an English shoe factory, and when he came to America he started at four dollars a day right off the bat. He sure don't have no hankering to go back." "My dad liked Canada better than he liked England, where he was born," said a worker who was himself a Canadian by birth, "and I like the good old U.S.A. the best of all. A working guy don't stand a chance wherever the English are." Evidence from those who claimed a knowledge of the facts served to strengthen the shipyard worker's disdain of Great Britain. But that disdain, with its foundations laid deep in the traditions of America and attached to the bedrock of the surviving antagonisms of the Revolutionary period, would have stood foursquare without supporting buttresses of observation and argument. The average worker cherished a picture of Great Britain as a king-ridden, nobility-serving country, whose workers could hold only the status of menials. He had not heard, and he refused to believe when told, that advances in social legislation had been achieved there in recent years and that the class barriers, which galled him although he only vaguely understood their nature, were rapidly disintegrating. England for him was still a land of dukes, duchesses, and lesser snobs, and it seemed all the more bitter to him that American lives should be spent in an effort to save this outworn system against which America itself had once had to fight.

Toward Russia the attitude was more complicated, since the Russian armies on their own independent front were on occasion indubitably successful. The charges that were brought against Great Britain, and the assumption of British dependence on American services in the conduct of the war, could not with any logic be used to cast discredit on the Russian nation. Although American aid in materiel was emphasized, Russia was nonetheless conceded to be a country with power of her own. Since success was admired for itself (even Germany in her days of triumph aroused for that reason a considerable esteem), Russia, so far as her armies advanced, was openly applauded. And yet the very power which Russia obviously possessed provided an additional basis for the distrust and the cocky belligerency which were also part of the typical shipyard reaction to this alien and almost unknown land.

The workers at Moore Dry Dock had some opportunity for direct contact with Russians, for Russian ships periodically were berthed at the yard for repairs. With the exception of a modern icebreaker presumably lend-leased from England, the Russian ships which I saw were small and ancient—the equivalent of the American or British tramps. Repair men working on them were full of scorn for their outmoded equipment and

unkemptness—the filth of the vessels was proverbial—
and freely admitted that they felt less than their usual
sense of responsibility for doing a sound job. One minor
boss amused a shipyard audience on several occasions
with boisterous tales of his efforts to put over inferior
material and craftsmanship on "them dumb Russians."
The crews of the Russian ships, moreover, were scrupu-
lously avoided as being strangers from a strange country and possible spies. The management added further
strength to these suspicions by delegating guards to observe the Russian sailors or girl stewards wandering
through the yards and to discourage any contact between them and the few workers who showed a desire
to fraternize. When I asked of a guard the basis of this
unfriendly policy, she said that most workers seemed
to want even more restrictions. "Girls complain to me,"
she said, "that they don't like to have those dirty Russian stewardesses in their rest rooms and that I ought
to keep them out altogether, and a woman told me just
the other day that there was a Russian sailor poking
around a ship all ready to be launched, and she was
sure that he was spying or maybe even figuring out some
kind of sabotage. Almost everybody just don't trust the
Russians."

It was the logical outcome of these various suspicions
that Russia should be selected in common shipyard
opinion as the appointed enemy of America for the next

world war. Influenced by the anti-Russian slant of the
newspapers which were most widely read, supposition
became almost a conviction long before the current
European conflict approached its close. Some workers
expected no decent halt to the war then raging in Europe
before the pell-mell plunge into a crusade against the
Soviet colossus. My own boss, a man of more than average capacity and wit, came to me in the early spring of
1944 with a tale which he accepted as completely valid,
the ultimate conclusion of which was war between the
United States and Russia by May 9. "The man who told
me this," he elaborated, "proved everything right out
of the Bible, and he said that we had gone to war with
Germany by mistake and that in another six weeks we
would find it out and then everybody together would
fight Russia, the real enemy of all the world."

A few of the workers were aware that a program of
social change was reportedly under way in Russia, the
aims of which, from the standpoint of the common workingman, were not entirely undesirable. I remember one
native of Oklahoma who, in the course of a tool-room
conversation, said most casually that in his opinion
Russia's social system had more to offer the workingman than America's. "They don't have any depres-
sions or unemployment over there," he concluded. But
shipyard understanding of the Soviet Union was, of
course, neither detailed nor profound. And, confusingly

enough, some who thought that a welcome rebellion against the power of wealth had come to pass in Russia also thought that Germany had attempted to institute a similar change and that it was through these efforts that she had fallen afoul of moneyed interests and Jews and had become embroiled in a disastrous war. For the most part, however, the differences in American and Russian social ideology, so far as they were known to the shipyard worker, served to augment his antagonism toward Russia: years of propaganda had found a fertile soil in his tendency always to think the worst of the new and the little known, and by now his concepts of Bolshevik irreligion, dictatorship, and sexual promiscuity had so flourished that he envisioned the approaching war against the Soviet Union, far more clearly than the conflict with Nazi Germany, as a crusade against evil.

Communism itself, the communism of the soapbox and the scattered pamphlet, he despised: it was an alien doctrine which had no right of immigration into the American political and economic scene. I was told of a worker who openly declared his communistic sympathies and was therefore shunned as if he were a leper. In all the months during which the newspaper sponsored by the local communistic group was offered to the home-going thousands of Moore Dry Dock, I saw no worker stop to buy a copy. The same group's booth near the gates, which was set up to sell and distribute pamphlets, went out of business in two or three weeks for lack of customers. Because of his aggressive refusal to investigate the suspected doctrine, the shipyard worker knew next to nothing of its actual content. Like many other words of prejudiced connotation with which his mind was well supplied, "communism" could nonetheless strike to his depths and arouse a compelling and bitter hate. Many viewpoints and activities were on occasion identified with communism. Advocacy of less inequality between the races was particularly subject to being considered communistic by those who felt that their privileges were thereby endangered. "It sounds like communism to me," one worker observed, "to let niggers join the same union with a white man." Unusual agitation for any political or economic issue was subject to the same charge. I once brought to the yard a petition urging passage of two Federal bills for the welfare of the blind, and as I requested signatures to it, one worker remarked without so much as a glance at the document, "I'm not putting my name to none of them communistic schemes." Because of my various political and union activities I was myself suspected of the brand, and everywhere I went with my registration blanks and my union literature I felt the shadow of the accusation behind me, although it never emerged into an open challenge. Any expression of approval of a foreign land was likewise assumed to be symptomatic of communism. At the time of the liberation of Paris I happened to remark to a man how thrilled I should be to walk through the streets of Paris on that day and join with the celebrating crowds. He looked at me, all puzzlement, and seriously inquired, "Are you a communist or something?" When the many aspects of the shipyard attitude toward communism are brought together and analyzed from their significant content, communism appears to represent within this area of opinion the strange, the new, and above all the threat of sudden change. The shipyard worker, just like the man of higher social rank, feared the intrusion of the new upon him, feared disturbance of the status quo, at least by force external to himself, because he feared the loss thereby of such privilege and property as he possessed. Hence he saw in communism a revolutionary movement indeed, but one which, by opening the gates to those yet lower in the social and economic scale than himself, would result in dreadful chaos—and his own undoing.

The tyranny of words over the shipyard mind is all the more obvious when it is noted that, unlike "communism," "socialism" was a fairly respectable term, admitted to represent a political and economic policy with many points in its favor. My own boss declared, with complete immunity from censure, that he considered himself a socialist and that his father had been a socialist before him. That "communism" might even-

tually come to enjoy a similar status of dignity and calm
acceptance was indicated by an isolated incident or two.
In the Marine Steamfitters, an avowed and well-known
communist became the moving spirit behind a successful program of union reform and regeneration, and
time after time was elected business agent. His keen-
ness and honesty overcame the doubts aroused by his
communism. "Sure, Al's a communist," one of his shipyard supporters remarked, "but I figure that his political opinions are as much his own business as his religion
is." I once overheard a worker praise Harry Bridges
and his contribution to the advancement of San Francisco labor, "although," the worker said, "I know he's
a communist." Another man who had been a member
of the C.I.O. United Automobile Workers' Union in its
organizing days in the Oakland area commented at
some length on the communists who, he averred, were
active in the union. "You got to have some communists
to make a union good," he concluded. "They're the guys
who stick their necks out, who aren't afraid to go to jail
if they have to, and who can't be bought off by the
boss's money. They've got their price—I guess everybody has,—but no boss in Oakland ever went high
enough to reach it."

The great institutional unity of the nation failed to
assume, even in time of war, a real and vital meaning
for the mass of shipyard workers; it is not remarkable,

therefore, that appeals for an international outlook and
world-wide sympathies, currently on the tongues of
statesmen, went virtually unheeded. Disdain of foreign
ways, fear of foreign ideas, and hatred of foreign power
dominated shipyard thinking so completely as to exclude all curiosity concerning peculiar peoples and distant lands. Shipyard views of alien nations contained,
no doubt, the elements both of isolationism and im-
perialism which a clever demagogue might activate in
either political direction; but without the stimulation
of external propaganda these attitudes constituted no
definite or articulate program. For the most part the
shipyard worker considered the schemes of statesmen
and diplomats, whether they talked of international cooperation, of nationalistic rivalries, or of wary with-
drawal of each nation into its own sphere of security,
to be beyond his influence and therefore not worth his
attention. They reserved only the right to a pervasive
suspicion of the motives of the leaders of nations and
to the gloomy conviction that, however the play began
or whatever its plot, the final curtain would find the common people of America paying the piper with their
sweat and blood.

Yet the actual hope of the shipyard workers was for
peace and not for war. Despite the fact that the war had
brought them unaccustomed prosperity and had cost
them comparatively little in return, since they had

escaped the worst in sacrifice, and despite the fact that their land had been untouched by the most terrible consequences of modern conflict, they yet believed that the happiest of tomorrows would be the day when the war should end and the time when war as a practice of society should forever cease. Yes, almost to a man, they hoped for peace with a hope stemming from the fervor of the Christian dream, a hope that had survived centuries of suffering in the desert of despair. But hope was not equivalent to sanguine expectation, and it fell far short of faith. Though the termination of the war was confidently expected almost any day, no one among those to whom I spoke seriously expected that war as an institution would thereby be abolished, no one seriously expected that the machinations of the statesmen would really establish world-wide unity. Speculation was already rife about the next enemy, the next battlefield, and the best ways of avoiding the perils of the inevitable next war.

SHIPYARD SOCIETY

❖ EMPHASIS, throughout this study, has been upon the factors of disunity which split group from group in mutual suspicion and antagonism. The disunity was real; yet the shipyard worker as I knew him was no misanthrope, no rabid individualist, resistant to all intrusion into his personal sanctuary. On the contrary, he invariably considered a large group as his own; if the group were white and male, it comprised at least potentially the largest single segment of the shipyard population. Within it, and particularly within smaller sections of it, such as the men working together in a craft, relationships of great friendliness existed.

Indeed, what most impressed the newcomer from the world of middle-class formality was the atmosphere of comradeship and intimacy which prevailed among the shipyard workers. Use of first names was one of the more noticeable external symptoms, but the internal substance of conviviality was also well developed. The stranger was not strange for long. His marital condition, the number, names, and ages of his children—and, preferably, pictures of each,—and the principal events of his life, such as the parts of the country in which he had lived or worked and the different jobs he had held, were common property soon after his introduction into the ship or gang, and he, in turn, quickly learned all

[215]

about his companions. Thereafter, momentous events—marriages, births, or deaths—were met with congratulations, advice, or sympathy, often with substantial aid if the occasion demanded.

In my first months at Moore Dry Dock, when numbers were fewer and certain social disruptions had not yet come fully into play, hardly a week went by without a collection for some poor fellow who had been injured, whose wife was ill, or who, for some other pressing reason, needed a bit of money and encouragement. In the first fairly close-knit group with which I worked, which was composed of about thirty men and women, no birth, marriage, illness, or death directly affecting any member occurred without appropriate response from all the others. Even I, isolated though I was by peculiarities of outlook, manner, and background, was once surprised and infinitely touched by the response of this group to a misfortune of my own. My mother, whom no one in the shipyards had ever met, was suddenly taken seriously ill, and when I returned to work, after being absent a week, with the news that she was at least expected to live, a sizable collection of cash was presented to me, with which to buy any bedside comforts I thought that she might need. "Everybody loves their mother," said the girl who handed the cluster of bills and coin to me, "and we want to make your mother happy with this little gift."

The mutual aid apparent in small working groups was appreciably expanded by the "friendly society" activities of the unions, though with greatest effectiveness only before unions achieved gargantuan size. The fraternal greetings and ceremonials were taken seriously by some of the older members, and for these the death and sick benefits and the visits to incapacitated brothers by punctilious delegations were among the most appropriate and important functions the unions performed. Requests for aid to a fellow member in need were frequently made through union channels and usually met with generous response. Donations of blood were sometimes sought for one or another member of a union who was critically ill and who could not afford the fees that blood transfusions cost; or it would be learned that the widow of a member was in dire financial straits, and a sum of money would be voted her from union funds. The Marine Steamfitters, by means of a small assessment on their entire membership, collected fifteen hundred dollars for the benefit of a member who had been blinded in an off-job accident. Questions were seldom raised over such charitable or humanitarian projects of the unions; convinced of the need, most of the members gave ungrudingly whatever was desired.

The generosity of the shipyard groups was aroused chiefly by personal appeal or by direct observation of personal need. The illusion usually created was that of a familial group coming to the aid of one of its own. Intimacy, brotherliness, and personal concern—this was the spirit which at once illumined and delimited that area of mutual aid the obligations of which the shipyard worker admitted to be valid and compelling. Institutionalized charity, on the other hand, which lacked the personal appeal, was customarily viewed with indifference or skepticism. The doubts that clustered around all large organizations—doubts about integrity of leadership, about the ultimate destiny of the money—seriously hampered the annual War Chest campaign. Many, prompted as much by pressure from company management as by the impulses of their own good will, gave the prescribed amount; but many others did not. One worker, whom I knew to be as capable as anyone else of the generosity in which the yards abounded, tore up his War Chest pledge card in disgust. "What do they think I am, a sucker?" he exploded. "Them rich dames who hand around the Christmas baskets don't get a single penny of my wages, I can tell you, to buy themselves new uniforms and station wagons." At no time did the proportion of pledges from workers in the crafts achieve the peak set by the front-office clerical and professional workers, whose attitudes, it may be assumed, were more greatly influenced by the philosophy of Lord and Lady Bountiful.

The emphasis on personal contact and familial intimacy is not to be interpreted as constituting approval of individual caprice. The customary gestures of helpfulness did not involve particular affinities of personality or spontaneous outbursts of affection, but were prompted by a definite system of ethics with ironclad rules. The present to the newly married worker or the purse collected for the bereaved widow were not tributes of high regard, but tributes to a need, and ultimately to the insecurity which placed both giver and recipient in a common peril. Anyone within the circle, when confronted by a suitable emergency, was eligible for such conventional aid, and everyone else was obligated to provide it. Some entered into the approved relationships with greater enthusiasm than others, but the code of friendliness was observed by all except a few malcontents, who were ridiculed and left to stew in their own bitter juice.

Only as the hordes of strangers with conflicting backgrounds poured into the shipyards did traditional loyalties relax somewhat and the vigor of the code begin to slacken. Collections for the unfortunate fellow worker became rarer and smaller. My union felt impelled at last to discontinue the sick benefit to its members because, it was insisted, the incoming throngs were ignorant of the principles of unionism, abused the benefit, and made it financially unfeasible.

The deleterious effects upon established intimacies of the working groups which resulted from the increase in size and variety of the shipyard population were most clearly demonstrated to me when, after my first year, I was transferred from the old East Yard to the West Yard, which was the product of the war. In the old yard the relationships among the workers, like the patterns of construction, were well established in tradition, and the newcomer was readily absorbed into a circle which still remained intact. In the new yard the unsettling influences of the war had freer play, and the stranger and his code of independence and suspicion were prominent in the social scene. To shift from the East Yard to the West was like moving from a small town with its definite lines of neighborliness to a metropolis where the individual is reduced almost to an ultimate denominator and stands alone. The transition was not quite so extreme, of course, but the groups that formed in the new yard were for the most part smaller and less compact than those in the old, as well as less convivial in spirit, and many a transferred craftsman continued for months to look back upon the old yard with nostalgia.

But whether in the old yard or the new, whether at the beginning of the boom or at its end, shipyard society, on the level of face-to-face relationships, remained extraordinarily friendly. Even representatives of the minorities—some women and some Okies, for

example—were willingly included in various confraternities of coöperation and good-fellowship. A mother
of three children, who was seriously injured in a shipyard accident, received one of the largest purses ever
collected from the workers. Only the members of a
markedly different race, most notably the Negroes,
were excluded from these informal societies of mutual
aid. With but one exception of which I knew—a Negro
cripple who, cup in hand, stood at the shipyard gates at
quitting time and was fairly well rewarded for his os-
tentatious humility,—shipyard generosity never crossed
the barrier between black and white.

Others who, like myself, had ventured in wartime
to depart from the white-collar world, were even more
impressed than I with the friendliness of shipyard people, since they were not distressed with the search for
broader unities which troubled me. One woman, most
of whose life had been spent in the art colony of San
Francisco, expressed an especial admiration for the
shipyard worker. "I wasn't at work on my new job,"
she said, "or mingling with this new kind of people for
more than a week or two before I didn't care if I never
returned to the life I had known. These shipyard workers are wonderful, I think; they're real and solid and
simple as the earth, and in being so intimately associated with the industrial foundation of our culture
they have come closer than any other group I know to

the basic human values—to friendliness, sincerity, and mutual helpfulness." Another worker, whose background was primarily academic, was similarly impressed. "In all my life before," she said, "I never knew such spontaneous friendliness as I have found in the first weeks of my job here. The men and women I work with don't just say 'Good morning' and pass me by: they inquire about my troubles, whether personal or connected with the job, and are always ready with good advice and offers of help. I couldn't stay a stranger if I tried." The vision of the shipyard worker evoked by such enthusiasts was not unlike the image of the Noble Savage, the intellectual darling of an earlier age and tradition, and the same sentimentality was responsible for both instances of exaggerated statement. But the worker's character must nonetheless be seen as at least in part composed of the traits which charmed immoderate admirers.

The friendly groups of the shipyard, in their dependence upon face-to-face relationships and the sharing of intimacies, partook of the substance of the family circle, as was recognized and admitted by many who had long been accustomed to such societies. One worker, pleasantly reminiscing of his previous job, remarked, "Us fellows at the plant were like a family. There wasn't nothing we didn't know about each other. We were just about as close as if we'd been real brothers in the blood." A bachelor of respectable years, whose previous stretches of work had been long and dull, expressed a special fondness for the job he had held for seventeen years before coming to the shipyards—keeping a perpetual inventory in the warehouse of a hardware company. I asked how he had borne the tedium. He answered, "After a year or two I got to know the other fellows round the place real well, and the girls in the office, too. We got to be like one big family after a while, and we had fine times together at our Christmas parties and on Sunday picnics in the country. For me, seeing that I wasn't married, it was more fun to go to work in the morning than it was to go home at night."

The family was the significant social unit for the shipyard worker; the relationships it embodied were the ultimate source of his code. The small group of husband, wife, and children constituted his basic and most compelling society, the measure against which all other types of society were computed when he would test their value. Between the family and himself he usually drew but slight distinction. One ambitious young fellow was fond of saying that his creed in life was getting ahead. "It's so much the worse for anybody who gets in my way," he proclaimed. "The world is run by selfishness, and I'm going to make the top by being just a little more selfish than the other guy." I asked him once how his philosophy of ruthless self-devotion would affect his family—whether they, too, might be trampled on in his efforts to achieve the goals he desired for himself. As amazed as if I had missed the central point of his argument, he replied that his wife and child were his own, and it was for them that he toiled, hoped, and if need be would give his life. "I know that if I work myself to death," he concluded, "as I'm likely to in trying to get ahead, my kid at least will have a better start in life than it was my luck to draw."

Though shipyard workers showed little interest in the broad issues of ethics, they respected definite commandments for the regulation of the familial system. A man was as good or bad as his practice of the family virtues; his acts possessed or lacked merit as they affected his family. The harshest words that one boss had for a member of his gang too often late to work were that he obviously had no regard for the security of his wife and children and was a poor provider. "His old lady sure ought to ride into him," the boss asserted, "losing money from his checks the way he does by being late about every morning—and him with four kids, too!" In a union election campaign the qualifications of an incumbent were challenged by members who charged, with abundant and apparently trustworthy documentation, that he had embezzled union funds and therefore deserved to be summarily removed. The members of the shipyard circle were busily reviewing the accusations when one respected oldster quashed their doubts by remarking, "What's the difference what he done? He's a good family man anyway, and that should be enough for you guys. After all, you can't blame a fellow for dipping in the till now and then and taking what comes easy if he's got a wife and kinds to support." A discussion with a minister was reported at some length to me by a worker, out of pride in his own position. "A minister asked me," he said, "how I could hope to be a Christian if I didn't go to church every Sunday and say my prayers at night. Well, I told him that being good to my wife and paying my gas bills on time was Christianity enough for me, and I didn't need to pray because I thanked God every day by working hard for the sake of my wife and kid." He then contrasted his behavior with a neighbor's. "He's the most church-going man in the neighborhood," he said; "he goes every Sunday, and during the week besides, and he gives a lot of money to the priest. But in between he's always getting drunk; he beats his wife, and he makes his kids go hungry and wear ragged clothes. He's sure religious, but he ain't my notion of a Christian man."

The shipyard worker tended to assume that the familial structure, with its solidity confirmed by eternal ties of blood, was the only secure basis for the close association of men. He tried, therefore, to equate other, larger groups with which he was affiliated, such as the unions or the working gangs, with the familial or kinship system. The pretense of brotherhood was unquestionably a dominant principle in the formation and preservation of all close-knit shipyard groups, and the degree to which this pretense was maintained was the primary determinant of the group's cohesiveness and the prominence of mutual aid within it. What the kinship idea possessed in intensity of attraction, however, it lacked in inclusiveness and breadth of content: the Christian doctrine of universal brotherhood had no substantial meaning to the shipyard worker. For him, a kinship group necessarily implied the existence of the non-kin, the stranger, for whom there were no provisions in the code of coöperative relationships. Thus his system of society was marked by definite boundaries beyond which friendly contact was summarily discontinued; it was, so to speak, a small and compact island around which raged a mighty alien sea. The causes of disunity among shipyard groups were many and varied; certainly the emphasis upon kinship as the single criterion and basis of the sound society was not the origin of disunity, nor was it the spirit which inspired disunity to persist. But the dependence upon the kinship system of relationships nonetheless contributed to the conflicts in that the scope of the concept was narrow and its boundaries sharply

drawn. Often enough, the very intensity of the shipyard worker's attraction to the idea of kinship, as the
eternal rock on which his world of friendliness and
tolerance was founded, was likewise a measure of the
antagonism and suspicion which he turned toward the
larger world outside.

The kinship idea further sustained disunity by providing no support for the institutions which might have
destroyed and superseded the divisions among competing groups. The union, the class, and the state, having as their cohesive substance not common blood but
common needs and goals, constituted species of society
different from the family. Being different, they were
weaker; their appeal to unity was much less compelling and their power to claim and hold the allegiance
of the individual much less strong. Some effort was
made to camouflage this fatal difference by establishing the pretense of kinship in a society that was
essentially institutional. The fraternalism of the labor
unions was such an attempt. It may also be argued that
the childlike patriotism of the shipyard worker, with
its respect for the flag and its sentimental tears when
the brass band played the national anthem, extended
only so far as the fiction of the protecting fatherhood
of the nation was maintained. But since a policy of
undifferentiated and universal inclusiveness was resisted by the kinship idea itself, even this method of

invigorating institutional unities and giving them substance in the eyes of the shipyard population was limited in scope. Consequently, regard for the union and
the nation remained pitifully small as compared with
attachment to the intimate group in which the shipyard worker felt at home.

THE CHALLENGE

𝕏 IN ANALYZING the narrow social sympathies of the shipyard worker, attention must be paid to the environment which affected his point of view, or which at least inhibited his developing any other. The factors extending his social horizon were extremely few; those which prompted him to remain in a confined and easily protected area, to constrict his social outlook, and to devote himself exclusively to personal relationships, were overwhelming. In the first place, he had behind him only a minimum of schooling, by which he had acquired the bare rudiments of such practical knowledge as would contribute directly to wage earning. From his schoolroom desk he gained no broadening ideas of more intelligent social living. Then, while scarcely an adult, he stepped on the treadmill of the imperious job, at which he was to work blindly and without enthusiasm to the end of his days. For eight or more hours a day, for five or six days a week, he tended one of the levers upon which a complicated industrial civilization depends, and though he came to know well the uses of his lever, he never came to know or appreciate or understand the busy structure of which it was a part.

Perhaps the shipyard worker had been a farmer rather than a mechanic, and day after day had walked in clodded furrows; or perhaps a housewife, waitress, or sales clerk drudging at one or another of a thousand repetitive tasks. Whatever routine the shipyard worker was accustomed to, he had been bound and enervated by it, and all save a useless modicum of his energy had been dissipated by the mere gaining of a livelihood. To him, his job offered little beyond the satisfaction of his fundamental need to survive; it was seldom enjoyed for itself, and it was hardly ever related to the accomplishments of society. "Nobody works because he likes it," a craftsman told me; "he works because, if he didn't, him and his wife and kids would starve to death."

The job, the discipline and morality which surrounded it, held the workman's life in narrow, grubbing ways, confined his wisdom, and restricted the scope of his social sympathies. In the endless round of working to eat and eating to work there was little to inspire any consideration of social unity or universal brotherhood. Instead, it was the small group, particularly the family, toward which the job was oriented: the job provided sustenance for the family, while the family provided purpose for the job. The job, moreover, essential though it was, was not always easy to get; the worker was too frequently confronted with competitors whose purpose, it appeared, was to deprive him of it. In periods of economic crisis every workingman became the enemy of every other, and group was arrayed against group. Thus the job itself compelled the shipyard worker to withdraw from any broad field of unity into the one secure place he knew— the small but heartwarming circle of personal and family friends.

The spirit and structure of his culture likewise discouraged the formation of a large social unity. In the first place, the world into which he was born, for all its democratic pretensions, still cherished sharp distinctions of class and caste which consigned him to the lowest category of all, that of the propertyless, wage-earning, common man. Realizing his inferior economic and social status, he was stimulated to magnify the lesser group distinctions within his own extensive category. His social vision was yet further limited by the dominance in American social philosophy of the precepts of nineteenth-century liberalism which proclaimed that public interest was most adequately served by each individual's primary concern with his own affairs. Although these precepts did not penetrate to the level of the shipyard worker as fully enunciated arguments or rationalizations for behavior, they established an atmosphere conducive to attitudes of isolation and narrowness. His society being obviously both hierarchical and competitive, he was continually reminded that its richest rewards went not to the Samaritan who bound a neighbor's wounds, but to the man who passed by on the other side.

The institutions of the shipyard worker's culture which might possibly have served as agencies of fusion were themselves so permeated with the prevalent philosophy of insularity and competitiveness that their function as unifiers was either hampered or nullified. The doors of these institutions were bolted against the masses of shipyard workers. The fortunate few inside were understandably reluctant to dilute their privilege by sharing it, and for every voice that urged the worker to break the barriers and participate in the affairs of his nation and his world a dozen voices shouted down such presumption. Few shipyard unions exerted much effort toward encircling their war-swollen memberships within the unity of the organization. Even the state was unable or unwilling to absorb shipyard workers into active citizenship. To be sure, it could maintain a certain discipline over them, and it exacted extraordinary services, especially in wartime, which they were powerless to withhold, but in no sense did it provide a successful challenge to more intimate loyalty, nor did it divert from traditional insularity and antagonism.

The distance which existed between institutions and familial groups was no recent or chance phenomenon; it was, instead, the product of a long historical process which had accentuated distinctions and confirmed them as traditional. Without debating whether or not the family grouping was the basic type of human society, one still finds evidence enough of the historical primacy in Western culture of a kinship over a non-kinship or political system of social organization. And it is apparent, too, that among primitive peoples today kinship groupings are the almost universal substance of the community. The kinship system has deep roots within the past and flourishes in the present; it is both time-honored and common.

Political forms of social unity, when viewed against the entire sweep of human existence, are seen to be extremely recent. The first states, in the modern sense of the term, are contemporaneous not with the first cultures but with the first civilizations, not with the first societies but with the first sharp division of these societies into the two categories of the few who rule and the many who are ruled. The rule of particular states has for the most part been imposed by the power of conquest upon subject and acquiescent people. By taking the road of war, states grew large and enrolled the populations of competing nations under their banners and their laws, but their horizontal extension over more and more of the earth was matched by no downward penetration into the deeds and thoughts of their citizens. Between the state and the subject, in fact, a gulf was militantly maintained in order that the manipulation of political power might be retained as a perquisite of the few.

As a consequence, the common people of all nations and all historical times have been compelled to retain the smaller, nonpolitical systems of society and the intimate group loyalties which were theirs long prior to the emergence of political control. Thus the state, however large its area of dominance and however firm its internal discipline, has customarily represented only a veneer of social unity beneath which narrow, personal loyalties continued as the real substance of society. In recent centuries the preachments of democracy have raised their challenge to conventional concentrations of power, and in some especially responsive regions of the earth have measurably diminished the distance between the people and their interests and the state and its policies. But even in America the gap is not yet closed, and to the extent that it exists, the common citizen, here the shipyard worker, must rely on the familial group.

What emerges from this analysis of social hostilities among a group of shipyard workers is not the usual antisocial man, the individual who resists inclusion into any community from sheer love of his own independence, but rather the person who has given his primary allegiance to one type of society, who continues to be held to that allegiance by most of the conditions of his life, and who resists, therefore, the claims of larger groups. The conflicts and tensions of the shipyards, when viewed objectively, are seen to arise not from the ravening impulses of antisociality, but from a too-narrow and too-stubborn loyalty and from a concept of society the structure and limits of which are so fixed in hallowed custom as to be resistant to new fact and circumstance. The shipyard worker appears at the last to be no more and no less social than his culture permits.

Only on the basis of such an interpretation of social attitudes can the possibility of improvement in them be predicated. The problem of change becomes, then, not one of completely reversing innate tendencies and instinctual reactions, but rather one of extending and redefining tendencies which already exist and which have indeed developed as fully as the culture has allowed. The problem becomes, ultimately, one of providing suitable conditions for the growth of sociality. The shipyard itself, in certain of its aspects, offered such conditions. Circled by its walls and fences, groups hitherto isolated were compelled to associate in a common task under common discipline. In the consequent disturbance of habit, tensions and hostilities were aroused, but some weakening of barriers between groups was also accomplished and a cross-flow of fellowship occurred. Even where adequate adjustments were not achieved, a promise for the future here and there emerged, and amid the dissonance of hatred and suspicion an occasional harmony was audible.

Many specific incidents have been cited from the shipyard story to indicate the malleability of the workers' attitudes. The fact must always be kept in the forefront of attention that despite the existence among them of group divisions and antagonisms the thousands of workers of the shipyard community did coöperate in the accomplishment of common tasks. The prejudices I encountered in my two years of shipyard experience, furthermore, were for the most part merely verbal in their substance; upon them was lavished the cheap coin of the spendthrift tongue rather than the more closely hoarded capital of deeds. These attitudes, of course, were far from shallow, temporary, or purposeless; given the proper pressures and encouragement, they could no doubt have activated pogroms as bloody as have ever afflicted society. But it is equally probable that, under another set of pressures differently directed and skillfully applied, they might have been so weakened and diverted as utterly to have lost their force for evil.

The shipyard, however, was a highly transient settlement; it was no more than a boom town which, clamorously born on one day, passed into silence on the next. Its influence as a social force was therefore limited, and its possibilities as a unifier of dissident groups were never fully realized. In the wake of the shipyard's departure can be found little evidence of permanent change in the conventions of group differences and antagonisms which were cherished by its workers, little evidence that the old familiar shape of things in surrounding communities has been greatly altered. For such, after all, has commonly been the character of boom towns. They come and they go, and they appear to leave behind only the lifeless relics of former habitation. Yet, for those who search, another heritage assuredly remains—the vision of what could be brought to pass in the land were steady, conscious, and sober-minded effort long enough applied to its resources.

INDEX

ERIC ARNESEN is Professor of History and African American Studies at the University of Illinois at Chicago, and author of *Brotherhoods of Color: Black Railroad Workers and the Struggle for Equality* and *Black Protest and the Great Migration: A Brief History with Documents.*

ALEX LICHTENSTEIN is Associate Professor of History at Rice University, and author of *Twice the Work of Free Labor: The Political Economy of Convict Labor in the New South.*

The University of Illinois Press
is a founding member of the
Association of American University Presses.

Composed in 10.5/13 Bauer Bodoni
with Futura Bold display
at the University of Illinois Press
Manufactured by Versa Press, Inc.

University of Illinois Press
1325 South Oak Street
Champaign, IL 61820-6903
www.press.uillinois.edu